Endorsements and Prophetic Words:

The Kingdom teachings of this book are not new. It's the message that a Jewish Carpenter brought 2000 years ago to a people who were oppressed and hurting. The message is as relevant today as it has ever been. It is "... good news of great joy which [is] for all people"! It's a message about a Daddy in heaven who loves His kids with an outrageous love, and wants that love to be unencumbered by man-made barriers; but it's also a message about power... power to change. It is a message about transformation on the inside producing transformation on the outside until "...the kingdoms of this world have become the kingdoms of our Lord and of His Christ". While the truths are not new, the momentum to recapture them is. If you are hungry for truth, I highly recommend this book.

> — Benjamin A. Burdick
> Director, Bethel BSSM School of Ministry—
> Chicagoland

A powerful voice for the Kingdom! Pinky has the ability to put words together in a way that opens up the scripture, and these words will speak to multitudes.

> — Steve Backlund
> Global Legacy / BSSM Leadership Deployment
> Author of *Victorious Mindsets, Cracks in the Foundation*, and *You're CRAZY If You DON'T Talk to Yourself*

Pinky is destined to be a history maker and a world changer!

> — Kevin Dedmon
> Bethel Freedom Team / Firestarters
> Author of *The Ultimate Treasure Hunt: A Guide to Supernatural Evangelism through Supernatural Encounters*, and *Unlocking Heaven: Keys to Living Naturally Supernatural*

I see Pinky as a semi-truck driver who has the ability to pull into Heaven, load up with the words and gifts and blessings that are there, and bring them back to distribute to us! His words are powerful.

— Connie Deulley
Senior Management Team, Bethel Valpo,
Chicagoland Prophetic Ministries and Author
of *Discovering the Voice of God*

This book has the power to turn a skeptic into a believer, a believer into a follower, a follower into a disciple, and a disciple into royalty. Prepare to be forever transformed.

— Mandy Hart
Executive Director – AppaPhil

Pinky has expressed a revelation of the true heart of the Father, which has the potential to take us from what glory that we have known into more glory and greater freedom in our relationship with God, and to ultimately lead us into truly becoming more like Jesus.

— Shanie Hinge
Director - KKI Central and Eastern Europe

Life is filled with seasons and seasons are all about change and transition. I recently experienced one of the greatest and yet most challenging seasons in my life. In preparation, God sent me Pinky and his wife... a godsend! They put their hands to the plow with me and with their voices they spoke constant words of encouragement. I am eternally grateful for their friendship and partnership in ministry. I am also thankful for their hearts ... two hearts with one desire ... to see heaven invade earth!

— Scott Whaley, Founder & Executive Director
Global Camp Initiative

THE SE7EN KEYS TO THE KINGDOM

Could there be more to life than
we've ever known?

Apostle Pinky

WESTBOW
PRESS®
A DIVISION OF THOMAS NELSON
& ZONDERVAN

WestBow Press books may be ordered through booksellers or by contacting:

WestBow Press
A Division of Thomas Nelson & Zondervan
1663 Liberty Drive
Bloomington, IN 47403
www.westbowpress.com
844-714-3454

ISBN: 978-1-4497-0810-8 (sc)
ISBN: 978-1-4497-0811-5 (e)

Library of Congress Control Number: 2010940421

Print information available on the last page.

WestBow Press rev. date: 04/21/2022

To the love of my life… my wife and ministry partner, Lissa

For the hungry ones…

Thy kingdom come, Thy will be done in earth, as it is in heaven.

Matthew 6:10 (King James Version)

Contents

Kingdom Keys

This image is of a prophetic mixed media painting on canvas that was created by Kimberly Harper. She writes:

I painted this during a season where God was showing me the depths of His love. I titled this painting *'You've reached a part of me that no one else can see'*. His love goes beyond logic and understanding, and unlocks the hidden places in my heart. In Him I am fully alive, always accepted, and loved unconditionally.

—Kimberly Harper
  Artist

My wife first saw this painting when she met the artist in Redding, California. She told Kimmie of this book, and how it had three keys as a cover image. As my wife was departing, Kimmie blessed her and our ministry by giving us the painting. It speaks volumes to us, and the image and creative force and thought behind it are the heart of this book, so there was never a question as to it being the lead image of the book.

—Pinky

This image may be freely downloaded for personal use at
www.kingdomcultureministries.org

Foreword

The Lord woke me up at 3:00 AM last week with a word from the Psalms that He told me was for Pinky. At the time I had absolutely no idea who Pinky was, or that he was in the process of publishing a book. I had met him very briefly at the Bethel School of Supernatural Ministry where my husband was attending. I was there auditing the class with him over the course of a few days. I wrote the word down that the Lord had given me, in order to give it to Pinky later in the day. As I shared the word, Pinky stood with tears streaming down his face, obviously deeply touched by the heart of a Father who loves His son and knows exactly what he needs to hear.

A few days later, Pinky called me as I was preparing to board a plane to Denmark, to ask if I would be interested in reading his book and possibly writing the foreword to it. I was quite surprised and honored that he would ask, and agreed to read it and pray about writing this foreword.

As I read, I became more and more impressed with the wisdom, the insight and quite frankly the "controversy" of it. I LOVE it! Pinky challenges us, as the body of Christ, to allow the Holy Spirit to remove the blinds from our eyes and reveal His truth to us. A challenge to look beyond our church, family and social culture; to view the reality of the Kingdom Culture that God so desires to reveal to us today. I am reminded of the passage in 2 Corinthians 3:18 *"But we all, with unveiled face, beholding as in a mirror the glory of the Lord, are being transformed into the same image from glory to glory, just as from the Lord, the Spirit."* Within these pages, Pinky has expressed a revelation of the true heart of the Father, which has the potential to take us from what glory that we have known into more glory and greater freedom in our relationship with God, and to lead us into truly becoming more like Jesus.

This book reveals the heart of a Father who is passionate about His children, and aching to reveal Himself to them and bring them into their true identity. Pinky writes of a Father that longs to pour out a love that brings healing and freedom from the pain of legalistic religion, and draws believers into their destiny as children of the living God.

This book is for everyone who wants more of God and more of His power at work in their lives. This book is for those who want more of God and less of religion. This book is for the hungry ones who know that there has to be more to Christianity than what they see and live every day, but don't know exactly what that "more" is, or how to find it. This book is for those who think they have enough of God already, and don't see what the big deal is. I challenge you to read this book through to the end. If you only open your heart enough to ask God to show you His Kingdom, this book will guide you down the road that will allow Him the freedom to reveal His will to you. Let Him take you from glory to glory. Jesus said that we would do greater things than He did when He walked the earth. You have a destiny in God that is waiting to be unfolded! There is always more!

I leave you with this word that the Lord gave me for Pinky. Why? Because it reveals the heart of a Father who loves His son enough to wake a stranger at 3:00 am in order to tell Him so. He would do it for you as well, and I pray that it will minister to your heart as it ministered to Pinky's.

Pinky,

The Lord, your rock and your redeemer says: *"The words of your mouth and the meditation of your heart are pleasing in my site. You are the apple of my eye and my son in whom I delight. The heavens shake as I rejoice over you! I am bringing you into your inheritance. I see the desires of your heart and they are in line with the inheritances that I will give you. I will pour out on you rich blessings beyond what you have asked or imagined! You were created for splendor! Nothing less! How my heart leaps with the knowledge of all that I have to lavish on you, my beloved son in whom I am well pleased.*

Shanie Hinge
Director - KKI Central and Eastern Europe

Preface

Christians who are hungry for the heart of God are tired of playing church. Like the true worshippers that were mixed among the Pharisees, they know in their hearts that there is more to service than programs, more to church than boring sermons, and more to life than the emptiness that they feel inside. They have cried out to God unceasingly for answers, and God has heard the desires of their hearts.

The answer has been in front of our faces and under our noses for millennia, on every page of the Bible, but God has kept it hidden away for us for such a time as this. God showed me the Kingdom revelation during the Jesus People movement of the 1970s, but it was not in His time to reveal it to the church.

That time has now come. Christians around the world are experiencing the revelation of the Kingdom. Because of the name *Kingdom Hall* that is used by Jehovah's Witnesses for their place of worship, some have confused Kingdom teachings as associated with them. It is not in the least. The Kingdom message comes directly from the teachings of Jesus Christ. The church has had everything backwards, and God is now turning her around and starting to prepare His bride. All of hell is quaking at Kingdom revelation, and all of Heaven is pouring out into the Earth. Jesus taught us to pray "Thy Kingdom come", and we are now seeing it come to pass.

You now hold in your hands the mystery of the ages, the reason for our existence, the explanation as to how the apostles were able to go from despair and doubt at the death of their teacher, to the boldness of conviction that they gave their lives for. You now hold in your hands the answers to the questions of mankind, for you are now holding the keys to the Kingdom. Prepare to enter a world that you have never before imagined.

Introduction

Have you ever been wrong about anything?

Think about this for a moment. Have you ever passionately believed in something, only to find out later that you were mistaken all along? How about a relationship? How about a love interest? Have you ever been in a relationship that you believed to be true, only to be hurt or to find out that you had been lied to? How passionately did you love? How deeply did you believe in the relationship, only to learn later that it was a lie? The reason that I'm asking such questions is to begin a process that requires *you* to think. It will continue throughout the book. This book is about many things. It's about God. It's about Christianity. It's about religion and relationships, truth and doctrine, love and hate; but the one thing that it's not about is an attempt to try to tell you what to think.

From a very early age, we are *all* told what to think by our parents. Once we start school, the teacher tells us the answers to the questions that we don't know, and we accept them. Even as we grow older and move into high school, and then perhaps on to college; we assume that the teacher is knowledgeable about the subject. Therefore, when the teacher tells us what to think about a particular set of rules or circumstances, we assume that he or she has the knowledge about that subject, and so we accumulate our knowledge.

As we grow older and enter into adulthood, we might choose a job. On the job, the boss tells us how things work and how we are to work with and around those things. Whether we watch a talk show on TV, or read a self-help book, most sources of information in the world try to persuade us or to tell us what to think. Most people who write, speak or communicate with others in some way do so because they have knowledge on a particular subject that they want to share with others. You can easily understand then, that it only makes sense for a writer or speaker who wants to convey his or her knowledge and/or sentiments in a book or speech, to attempt to tell you what they know. The emphasis is on their thoughts about a particular subject. They have assumedly studied the subject, and have come to their own conclusions about it. Their ultimate goal is to explain to you what they think or believe, in an effort to get you to think or believe the same thing.

Of itself, that's not necessarily a bad thing. It's not necessarily a bad thing to teach children what to think. The point I'm making however, is that our entire lives are spent being told what to think. The goal of this book is not to tell you what to think about any subject that is included. Instead, it's my goal to show you *how* to think. As you read further along in this book, you'll discover that I don't say "Here is what I believe", and then try to put forth the arguments to convince you to believe it also. Instead, I have developed a knack for quoting Scripture, and making statements and observations that require you to think about the possible outcomes, and make some of your own decisions. I have found that, at least for my own way of learning, once I can put two and two together and draw my own conclusion; I'm not only happier and more confident with the resultant, but it stays with me longer than if somebody simply tells me what they believe the answer to be.

Please don't misunderstand me. I am not trying to insinuate in the least that you don't know how to think for yourself. I don't believe for a moment that I have a higher intellect or a deeper understanding that I have to impart into you somehow. I'm simply stating a fact about our acquired knowledge. Once you think about it, you realize that a lot of our knowledge has been obtained from people telling us what to think. It's a truth that you've always known subconsciously. I'm only putting it into words to focus it into consciousness.

The point is not that you don't know how to think for yourself... of course you do. It's my intention though, to cause you to start consciously thinking about many things that you might already know to be true in your heart that have not quite yet worked their way into the head. If you apply the concepts of this book, your life will be transformed and changed for the better in ways that you can never imagine right now. I realize the magnitude of that statement, and I promise you that it's not made lightly or with frivolity; for within the words of this book hang the keys to the Kingdom.

How to read this book

The very first time that you read this book, read through it from beginning to end without skipping around the chapters to read one that sounds more appealing to you. The book has been carefully and thoughtfully laid out with chapters in a particular order for a very specific reason. The chapters slowly build precept upon precept, and none should be skipped over; as that would only create confusion upon reading future chapters. At times I will ask you to perform a task. I do so for a reason, and it's important for your journey down this path that you complete the tasks. Also, most chapters have been deliberately kept relatively short. I realize that many don't like to read books in this day of instant electronic communication, and those who do read do not have a lot of time to do so. It would be my suggestion to read no more than one chapter and then walk away from the book for a time to think about, pray about and research what you just read. There are going to be chapters that will be challenging to you, as some may cause you to rethink things that you have always believed to be true.

Remember that many who lived in medieval times thought the world to be flat. They might have believed so with a passion, and argued their belief to the point of exhaustion. Nevertheless, no matter how passionately they believed... they were wrong. This should go to show you that it doesn't matter how many people believe something is true, or how passionately they believe it. If it's not true, even a deeply held fanatical belief is not going to cause it to become truth. In other words, I'm giving you the old adage of 'just because you believe it doesn't make it true'.

Speaking of the myth of the flat Earth, didn't you learn in school that the Earth being flat was a belief widely held during the Middle Ages? That's how my school taught it. I was always taught that, even toward the end of the Middle Ages when Europeans began sailing toward the new worlds, that some were afraid that their ship would eventually fall from the edge of the Earth. I was taught that, but now I know that it's simply not true. There were hardly any who believed that the Earth was flat after the 5th century, much less into the 15th century. The few if any that held to a flat Earth belief into this time period were only the most extremely uneducated element of society.

Here's another trivial tidbit for you that you may not know. How many times have you heard that turkey contains tryptophan, and is the reason that people get sleepy after a big Thanksgiving Day meal? I've heard people repeat it over and over. However, the facts are that while turkey does contain tryptophan, and while that particular amino acid has proven to have sleep inducing qualities (as well as breaking down into serotonin and melatonin); the small amount of tryptophan that is ingested in conjunction with the large amount of food consumed, makes it an impossible candidate as a sleeping aid. There are other foods that can contain as much or more tryptophan than turkey, including burgers, pork and cheese. Have you ever heard of anyone passing out from eating a grilled cheese sandwich?

While we're on this fun subject of things that people have been taught that simply aren't true… Most people learned in school, or from TV, books or movies; that witches were burned at the stake in Salem Massachusetts in 1692 during the Salem witch trials. While there *were* 20 people found guilty of witchcraft that were subsequently executed, not one was burned. Why? In the new colonies it was unlawful to burn a human being. During a visit to Salem, I discovered the true fate of the accused witches. One was crushed to death by huge stones, and the other 19 were hanged.

Have you ever been told that you must wait 30 minutes after eating before going swimming to avoid getting the cramps, and possibly drowning? Weren't you always taught in school that the body only has five senses (sight, hearing, touch, smell and taste)? Those who know someone that might have tended to run afoul of the law have surely heard it proclaimed for a fact that (at least in the United States), a policeman must answer truthfully when asked if he is a cop. While all of these might be believed by a majority of the populace… they are all simply myths. None of them are true.

If you overeat and then try to go swimming, the worst that would happen is that you could possibly become a bit uncomfortable. There is that rare person who might develop a cramp, but it would be a very mild one that would definitely not deter swimming. The fact is there has never been a case of someone eating, going for an immediate swim and drowning because of the cramps. As for the senses in your body, there are at least nine and perhaps as many as 21 depending on exactly how you define a sense. Any medical personnel will be able to tell you that along with the five senses that you know about off the top of your head, there is also thermoception (the sense of temperature), nociception (the sense of pain), equilibrioception (the sense of balance), and proprioception (the sense of perception). Most researchers include the senses of hunger and thirst, and there are many more, depending on who you ask. To be considered a sense, there need only be a sensory organ that assimilates external data and submits it to the brain.

As for the policeman having to identify himself, people confuse that with the laws against entrapment. A policeman may not coerce an individual into a crime, but there is no law that requires a policeman to identify himself as such, and a failure to do so is in no way considered coercion.

I have heard throughout my entire life, that upon learning that her subjects were starving to death because of famine and the exorbitant cost increase of bread, Queen Marie Antoinette made the cruel statement *"S'ils n'ont plus de pain, qu'ils mangent de la brioche"* which roughly translates into: "If they have no bread, let them eat cake". Weren't you always taught that Thomas Edison invented the light bulb and that Napoleon Bonaparte was short? There's even a colloquial term for a short-stature inferiority complex. It's referred to as the *Napoleon complex*.

Those are some of the things that we have been taught, but are they accurate? Here are some of the various facts: After the storming of the French Bastille, the royal family was imprisoned. King Louis XVI was exiled and vicious false rumors of every type sprung up against Marie Antoinette simply because she was an easy target. Infuriated by the royal family's extravagant lifestyle in Versailles while the rest of France faced a devastating depression, many of her disgruntled subjects began to slander her with every imaginable wrongdoing. Many falsehoods were attributed to Marie that eventually led to her execution by guillotine; however there is no historical evidence whatsoever that Marie Antoinette ever uttered those words. If she actually did, they were definitely not her own and not original to the plight of the French. The true author of the phrase might well have been Jean-Jacques Rousseau. It is included in his _Confessions_, the tome that scholars consider to be the first secular autobiography. It becomes easy to understand why we today would continue to attribute that phrase to Marie Antoinette, when so many of her own contemporaries believed the rumor.

As for Napoleon Bonaparte, he wasn't 5'2" as is recorded by many a historian. The reason for the confusion stems from the fact that the French inch of Napoleon's time was actually longer than the British inch. Napoleon stood 5'2" tall as measured by the French inch. The British equivalent would be 5'7" tall. While this might still sound a short stature by today's standards, people were actually much smaller at the turn of the 19th century. In France, 5'7" would actually have been the average height for a man. Here's a bonus myth for you: there has never been a study that would indicate a short statured man to be particularly aggressive, but there have been studies that disprove that theory. That means, ironically, that not only was Napoleon of average height (and therefore not aggressive because of short stature), but what has always been referred to as the _Napoleon Complex_ doesn't exist either.

As for Thomas Edison's invention, the electric arc lamp was actually invented by the Englishman Humphrey Davy 70 years prior to Edison's 1880 light bulb. Another British inventor by the name of Frederick DeMoleyns found a way, in 1841, to pump out the air from a glass bulb that contained a carbon burner. This gave it longer life, albeit still impractically short. Inventors had known how to make a light bulb for decades, but it just could not be made practical. Edison assembled a team of inventors at his Menlo Park workshop that worked tirelessly for years to find the proper combinations of elements that would make a light bulb practical for the everyday user. His team finally discovered carbonized bamboo to be the perfect element. So truth be told, Edison did not invent the light bulb nor did he invent the process by which it is built. More than likely, it was not even he that discovered the better filament; but one of his workers. For the most part, Edison was just in the right place at the right time, and was financially able to employ people who were working on the right project.

After the manuscript of this book was completed, I returned to it because of news articles that are now purporting that one of the most popular of all dinosaurs, the Triceratops, probably never existed. It's now believed that those skeletons are of the immature Torosaurus. So, how many of the things that we *know* that we know are even correct? I do hope that you've enjoyed learning these fun facts about some of the myths that we hold to be true; but there is a crucial reason why we are learning them. It's all part of beginning the method of learning *how* to think, rather than being told *what* to think. Now it's time to put the book down for a while to go and do some research. Surely there's at least one of the statements that I've made that you just absolutely know for a fact I'm wrong about. After the research, and maybe a cheese sandwich, feel free to pick the book back up again. Just remember... no skipping around. There are many reasons that the chapters occur the way that they do. Start with chapter 1 and read each chapter in numerical order. After each chapter, take a break to collect your thoughts, research or get another grilled cheese sandwich.

Chapter 1
Mayday!

This story simply amazes me, and I would like to share it with you.

Friday night

May, 02, 2008 10:00 pm

My sister died last night. This could be the shortest story of all time, because... that's it... that's the end, isn't it? I mean... when you read a tear-jerker that develops a character that you grow close to, that you become friends with, that you fall in love with, it rips your heart when you read that line "...and she died in the night." The story ends, and you walk away with tears rolling down your cheeks the way that they're rolling down mine as I write these words. You get this same indescribable lump that is, at this moment swelling in my throat and wanting to release itself into a blinding and deafening explosion of emotion as I just realized that... as I write these words and glance at the clock... twenty-four hours ago I spoke to my sister. Now she's gone.

I'm writing this in real time so that you may know my mind while it is fresh and my exposed heart as it is overwhelmed. I'm writing this so that you might share this amazing story with me as it unfolds; because this is not the end... this is only the beginning. The beginning of something that cannot be completely comprehended at this time, for the fact that I'm not recalling a past event with the perspective of 20/20 hindsight and the succor of being able to see the outcomes of all the different directions that this news will spiral into. For I'm right here with you, right now as you read. I want you to know what I know at this moment in time. I want you to feel the rollercoaster of waves that are crashing all around me. One will slam me to the bottom and drag me along the jagged terrain until there is no breath left in me. As the black kaleidoscope collapses around my eyes and I fear that I'll not draw another breath, the next wave pulls me back to the surface. Here it's sunny and warm and beautiful and glorious. Floating in this breeze is a Heavenly experience full of enlightenment and a peace that passes all understanding. As I momentarily bask in this beauty and marvel at this tranquility, I'm also forced to brace myself against the next wave.

Saturday morning

May, 03, 2008 7:00 am

Today is not the typical May morning. It's cold and grey and raining. I just looked over across the Ohio River, and I can't even make out the shore line for the misty haze that blankets the water. As I write these words I become one with the day. My sister has passed away at age 38 and I still don't understand why. There has not yet been an autopsy, so I don't know if it was a drug overdose or a heart attack. Maybe it was both, maybe it was neither. If drugs were involved, was it intentional or accidental?

Although our entire family is in shock and in disbelief, in the same breath, we each hold our tongue against that unspeakable thought. We each, in our own way, have been preparing for this moment for years now. Tammy abused her body to the point of death so many times before. She lived her life in a perpetual drug induced haze, with inner demons that caused her to cut herself so deeply, that several times it went clear to the bone. Her bipolar, manic depressive mood swings have caused her to try to commit suicide so many times in the past. I can't begin to recount the times when I received that late night call that my sister was once again rushed to the local ER. Once more she was lashing out against the physical pain and the mental and spiritual torture, by attacking the very body that held her captive to it.

It seems that every family has the one proverbial black sheep somewhere along the line. Every family but mine, that is. It's not so much that Tammy was the lone black sheep of the family, as it is that I'm the lone white one. The majority of my family decided to have a party last night that included snorting Oxycontin, because in their words, that's what Tammy would have wanted. It's far too early in the morning to know if they all pulled through unscathed.

The chain of events

I want to relate to you a chain of events that has been revealing itself over the last couple of days. Had any one of these events not occurred, or had one occurred a few minutes earlier or later than the other, then the chain would have been broken, and the story would have ended with the first sentence of this writing. The fact that each and every event happened exactly when and how they did, reveals and speaks to me of intelligent design. The resultant conclusion and the order and timing of events are so astronomically beyond the realm of chance as to make it a mathematical impossibility. I used to believe in coincidence, but I no longer do. If I were writing this as a novel, it wouldn't sell because nobody would believe the fantastic series of events. But it's not a novel. I'm not writing this from my head, but from my heart. I'm going to write the events of these last two days, word for word, as they transpired.

The story actually began on March 9, 1994 when a photo was taken. That photo was then put away and lost for over fourteen years. Now, flash forward to 2008. As I am writing this down it is now Saturday, May 3, 2008, but I want to take the reader back two days to May Day Thursday May 1, 2008. The events are fresh in my mind as I write, for it was only two days ago.

It was early in the day on Thursday. Memaw had been cleaning out her house and going through some old moving boxes. In one of the boxes was a crumpled paper sack that she discarded. A few minutes later, she had no idea why she suddenly felt as if she needed to retrieve that bag from the trash that had been set out for collection. "Something told me to get that bag and look in it", she recounted to me. Minutes before the trash collection trucks arrived, she removed the crumpled up paper bag from the trash and opened it. In the bottom of that bag, she discovered and retrieved an envelope that no one had previously seen for well over a decade. It had her daughter Lissa's name written on it, so she took it inside the house in order to give it to Lissa the next time they were together. Janette, newly married into the family, was staying with Memaw. Curious about what was

3

inside of the envelope, she surreptitiously opened it, looked at six photos contained inside, and quickly replaced them.

Lissa's brother-in-law, Wayne, had been in the hospital for a couple of days. Doctors didn't seem to know what was going on, but he was on the verge of renal failure. Somewhere around the middle of the day on Thursday, Wayne took a turn for the worse. From the reports that were given, we believed that his life could be at stake. For that reason, we put calls out to several different states for several different prayer chains to be initiated on his behalf.

Somewhat later that Thursday evening, Lissa wanted to go to the hospital to be with her little sister, Trae, and her brother-in-law Wayne, to offer prayer and whatever other help and comfort that she could. Memaw is mother to Lissa and Trae, as well as three older siblings: Angie, Tammy, and Steve. They all call her Memaw because their kids call her that. Trae and Memaw do not have a close relationship at all, so Lissa had no idea why Trae would have called Memaw to ask if she would come to the hospital. Once again, as Trae stated it, "something" told her to call Memaw. It was a very odd request from Trae when she phoned Lissa to ask her to pick up Memaw on the way. It was so out of character that Lissa became truly concerned about Wayne's condition. Lissa agreed to bring Memaw, but had to drive well out of her way in order to do so. That might not have sat perfectly well with her, as she was doing all that she could to get to the hospital as soon as possible.

Eternally the good sister and daughter, Lissa drove several miles out of the way to pick up Memaw. As she was getting into the car, Lissa was burning up her cell phone leaving messages with this church and that one, frantically ringing everyone she knew that had a church and a prayer chain to put Wayne's name on. Memaw brought with her the envelope that had been rescued from burial in a landfill only hours earlier. She tried to give it to her daughter, but Lissa just motioned to her to place it in the glove box. She was paying little attention to Memaw, as her focus was on both her phone conversations and getting to the hospital to be with her sister and brother-in-law in their time of need.

While en route to the hospital, Memaw asked Lissa to call Tammy's husband Dennis, to give him the bad news about Wayne. Several months earlier, Memaw's daughter Tammy had moved out of the Ohio Valley and down to Slidell, Louisiana with her husband Dennis. Wayne was a hunter and Dennis was a hunter. At least in that sense, they were a bit more like brothers than brothers-in-law, and Memaw knew that Dennis would take the news hard if anything happened to Wayne.

On Thursday night at 10:00 pm Eastern Standard Time, Lissa placed a call to Slidell in order to speak with Dennis, only to find that he was not at home. He had gone out to the store a little earlier. Lissa's sister Tammy was on the other end of the phone. Since she had moved away, the sisters no longer got to see each other or talk to each other as much as they would have liked. Lissa always enjoyed talking to the elusive "straight Tammy" and was pleased to hear her articulate, nearly straight sister on the other end of the phone. Lissa tried to tell her about Wayne, but Tammy had just had a grandson and she was so excited about it, that Lissa let her talk on. She enjoyed listening to Tammy being so happy and proud. Tammy spoke of plans to go see the baby as soon as possible and all the things she wanted to buy for her grandchild. She must have bragged about the baby for about ten minutes before the conversation turned to Wayne. She was concerned of course, and asked how their little sister Trae was holding up. Lissa asked Tammy to inform Dennis, and then asked Tammy if she would pray. She said that she would, and just before getting off the phone, Lissa said to her again, "Don't forget to pray." Tammy replied, "OK, I love you. I'm going to pray right now" and she hung up the phone. The time at which the phone call ended can only be estimated at between 10:15 and 10:20 pm EST. According to Dennis, he arrived home at approximately 10:25 pm Eastern Standard Time, to find Tammy comatose on the couch. Believing her to be in yet another of her drug induced sleeps, he carried her to bed and then went back to watch TV.

On the early Friday morning of May 2, 2008 at 6:30 am, Trae arrived at her sister Lissa's home in tears. She had called a countless number of times, but Lissa and her husband were still asleep and didn't hear the phone. They were awakened by the frantic pounding on the door, and Lissa opened the door to a sobbing Trae. Lissa and her husband expected only the very worst news imaginable... Wayne had died from renal failure. What else could bring her sister sobbing at her doorstep this early in the morning?

Lissa braced herself for the shock of actually hearing the words spoken; but when Trae finally got the words out... their cold slap stung Lissa's face and pierced her heart. "What do you mean Tammy?... What do you mean Tammy?... What are you saying? It's not true!!!"

At 7:00 am Eastern Standard Time, Lissa's husband called Tammy's husband Dennis, hoping to discredit the news. Dennis said only "yes, it's true. She died sometime last night, and I'm leaving the house right now. I can't stay here. I can't believe it. I just can't believe it... but she's really dead." The phone clicked. Thinking that Tammy had simply overdosed, Dennis thought that he had been the last to speak with his wife just a few hours earlier. Thinking that Tammy had been with Dennis Thursday night, and that he had contributed to her partying and overdosing, Lissa never again wanted to talk to Dennis, and did not call back. Therefore nobody knew the all-important time lines.

Later in the day, Lissa was praying for peace and understanding as to why this had happened. After learning from her husband that Dennis would be out of the house all day, she was led to call Tammy's house to hear her sister's voice one last time on the answering machine. She dialed the number and waited for the answering machine, but Dennis had briefly returned to the home at that moment to retrieve something, and answered the phone. She wanted to spew venom at him for letting her sister die, but by the grace of God, held her composure.

After a very brief and tenuous conversation, Lissa said goodbye; and then, only as an afterthought, just as she was about to hang up, Lissa mentioned that Wayne was doing better. In fact, Wayne had made a miraculous recovery that started only minutes after Lissa called to tell Dennis that he could possibly die. "What do you mean?" Dennis queried. Stunned that he didn't seem to know anything about Wayne, Lissa asked "Didn't Tammy tell you?"

This initiated an entire conversation in which both Dennis and Lissa learned the truth about the time line of events. Lissa now knew that she had spoken to Tammy only minutes before she was found, and that the last thing that Tammy had done was gone to the Lord in prayer.

Upon learning that, a peace washed over Lissa. She had known in her head that Tammy had prayed, because Tammy would never have told her that she was going to pray had she not been; but she thought that Tammy had then turned her back on the Lord to party. Now, however... she believed in her heart that Tammy had not only prayed for Wayne, but also prayed for forgiveness, minutes before she slipped away.

Lissa's mind was racing while she was trying to fathom what was now a very real possibility, Tammy could be in Heaven right now! She had to call Misty in Texas with this incredible glimmer of hope that shone through the bleak devastation of the day. Misty is Lissa's sister on her father's side. As Lissa was telling Misty about the revelation of Tammy's possible redemption, she and Misty began laughing and crying, thinking about Tammy and their Dad (who had passed on several years earlier) doing silly things in Heaven together, like riding Harley Davidson motorcycles. Suddenly, another revelation hit her. Lissa thought of her daughter Angel that had died in childbirth. As the cries of pain became tears of joy, Lissa said "Oh, Misty, I believe with all my heart that Tammy is in Heaven right now with Angel." Although she whole-heartedly believed it to be the truth, her deepest desire was that everyone could know this truth as well. "Jesus," she silently prayed, "please help me to find a way to show others this revelation that you've given me!"

Seconds after she spoke those words, a call came in on the other line from Janette. Lissa said goodbye to Misty and switched lines. Janette began cautiously, "I don't know if this is a good time, but do you remember that envelope that Memaw put in your glove box?" She then proceeded to inform Lissa of the pictures that she had seen the previous day. Lissa couldn't believe what she was hearing! She ran out to the car at breakneck speed to retrieve the photos from the glove box. She opened the envelope only to find a photo that she had never seen before. One that she never knew existed. One that was taken fourteen years earlier on the saddest, most heart-wrenching day of her life, and then miraculously appeared in her life in split second timing, fourteen years later.

The photo in the envelope that had been discarded in the trash… the photo that was minutes away from certain destruction in the steel jaws of the garbage truck until "something" told her mom to retrieve it; the photo which one could remember being taken… was a photo of her sister, Tammy lovingly caressing Angel's head in her hand. Lissa had asked for some type of sign from the Lord that Tammy was in Heaven with Angel, and the Lord gave her a photograph!

Now, Lissa doesn't believe that Tammy is in Heaven with only her dad and daughter, as there were many loved ones in Tammy's life that had passed on before, including some of Tammy's own children. This request of the Lord, made by Lissa, was to assure her that Tammy was with Angel, and also with the Father in Heaven. Our glorious God, in split second timing, provided the answer she needed.

Wayne was doing fine by this time. Calls were then made to update the various prayer chains that had been initiated for Wayne about his condition, and only then was it learned that, under different peculiar circumstances, not one of the prayer chains for Wayne had ever been set in motion in Kentucky, Ohio, West Virginia, Kansas, Missouri, or Alaska. It's never happened before that any one of those prayer chain requests went unheeded... but this time, believe it or not, not one of them were set into motion. Remember, Lissa was leaving messages all over, but she never spoke to anyone. We now can only conclude that prayer chains were not needed for Wayne, as he was healed once Lissa laid hands on him in prayer. The Lord then used Wayne's illness as an opportunity for Lissa to call her sister and encourage her to open up a conversation with the Father. A conversation that He knew needed to happen at that moment. Lissa believes that Tammy had already taken the fatal pill before the two had spoken, but it had not yet kicked in. God knew that time was of the essence for this conversation to take place, so Lissa's call had to happen at an exact moment. Only a few minutes earlier or later would have yielded an entirely different outcome.

All things work together for good for those who love the Lord. Lissa believes that Wayne's illness was part of that work. We don't believe for an instant that God caused Wayne sickness in order to accomplish His goal of reaching out to Tammy, but we do believe that He *used* it for the greater good. After the goal was established, the Lord healed Wayne.

It was revealed to Lissa that this story was to be written down and told to others. "That's a great story" you might say, "but I've heard a lot of similar so-called miraculous sounding stories on the Internet before that never seem to be able to be validated. Who is this person Lissa? Who wrote the story and how can you prove that it actually happened? "Well, my friend, the story did not come off of the Internet. I know firsthand that the story is accurate and factual, because I'm the one that wrote these words the night after Tammy's death. Lissa (pronounced Lisa) is my wife. We were both going through the events and emotions together, but once I sat down to commit the story to posterity, I wanted to write in the third person from my wife's perspective. At the time, she was barely able to think... much less write. I'm greatly indebted to her for, among so many other things, her strength and courage in being able to read through this chapter and add some of the detail that I wouldn't have known. She has in her heart to write a book about the fascinating story of Tammy's life and death, and I hope that this chapter will inspire her to do so.

This story is word for word accurate and true, but it can't be used as a doctrinal debate of what happens when you die, who goes to Heaven, how will we look when we get there, etc. Try to move beyond that. Try to move beyond doctrine, beyond belief or non-belief. This is not a lesson on understanding Scripture; it's an event that shows that God wants to communicate with us. He wants to get down on our level and meet us wherever we are. He wants to give us comfort and understanding. He wants us to have validation, peace and strength; but more than anything else, He wants to show us love.

Lissa had so many questions. We all had so many things running through our minds. Everything seemed wrong. Our world was being turned upside down and shaken. We needed strength. We needed hope. We were crying out to the Lord for answers... and He gave us one.

The Answer

This photo is the one that Tammy's story was written around. The photographer is unknown, but the photo has been retouched at Lissa Pink Studios. It appears here, along with the story, as testament to the comfort of the Holy Spirit, and in memory of Angel and Tammy Lynn

This image may be freely downloaded for personal use at ww.kingdomcultureministries.org

Chapter 2
What does it all mean?

If you subscribe to coincidence, you would have to admit that Tammy's story is an unbelievably amazing set of coincidences spanning a decade and a half that eventually culminated in, and came down to split second timing. It's even more amazing once you know that there were a lot of other events that wove themselves into an out of the happenings of that time that showed even further that this was not a series of random events. They were most meaningful to my wife and myself and our loved ones, but would not necessarily be meaningful outside of our family, and were therefore not included in the story. Perhaps one day the full story can be told.

This is not the only story that I could tell you about so-called coincidences. There are so many others happening in and around our lives. I will relate a couple more later on in the book, but there are other books on the market that deal with this subject exclusively, if you are interested. Author SQuire Rushnell has written a series of books on these topics that may be accessed from: www.whenGodwinks.com.

The main reason that I wanted to include the painful, tragic, joyous recounting of Tammy's story is, once again, to get you to think. I could tell you that there is a spiritual world happening all around us that is more real than what we know to be real about our world, but of course, you could say that it would only be my opinion. I could tell you that there are angels at our beck and call that are waiting to be released, waiting to interact, waiting to fulfill their destiny; but again, you could see that as pie-in-the sky wishful thinking. I could tell you that the Creator of the universe has a desire to communicate with us on a daily basis, and uses all types of situations and vehicles to do so, but you can also counter with your belief that God doesn't have time or resources to deal with us on such an infinitely small individual level.

To that end, I have presented Tammy's story. So what does it all mean? Could it be only coincidence? The definition of coincidence is: *The occurrence of events that happen at the same time by accident, but seem to have some connection.*

The definition of accident is: *An unforeseen or unplanned event.*

It's obvious that the events of Tammy's story are connected. Were they random and accidental, they would indeed fit the definition of coincidence. The word *coincidence* and its definition are man-made words to explain something that we don't understand. If we don't understand it, how do we know it to be occurring in an accidental manner? The events that we refer to as *coincidental* occurred long before the word itself ever existed. Man just put a word to the event in order to better enable himself to refer to it.

'G-o-d' is a man made word as well. Just because we know the word and the dictionary's meaning of the word doesn't mean that we understand who or what God is; nor will our alteration, manipulation or perception of the word change who or what God is. In other words, God by any other name is still God. These events (which most refer to as coincidences) continue happening in our lives. They will continually manifest regardless of what we call them. Therefore, my wife and I have renamed them. We now refer only to *God-incidences*.

Had Tammy's story happened to someone else, and had that someone tried to convince me that the events that happened within and around the story occurred simply by accident and that they were mere coincidences; I would be dumbfounded. I am a realist. When I look back over the events, and see how the different scenarios could have happened in thousands of different orders and in hundreds of thousands of different combinations, at multiple millions of different combinations of dates and times which, when all combined could have played out in an unfathomable number of different ways; and then when I factor in the human elements… I would be a fool to place odds on the likelihood of each of those events happening in the exact, precise chronological order in which they happened in the course of time. To look at unfathomable odds in a different light: I understand that someone is going to win the state lottery, but if you want me to place odds of one particular person winning not only the state lottery, but simultaneously the lottery of two other states as well, all on the same day... I would have to back away.

In other words, being a realist, it's easier for me to believe in some type of divine intervention than it would be to believe that all of those separate and unrelated events throughout the course of years actually all came together to work towards a final result simply by random chance or accident.

Does this mean that God causes death, or chaos, or devastation and destruction to see his will accomplished? Absolutely not! Did God create those things? That's a loaded question. God is the creator. Man did not create evil, nor did Satan. We are but created beings ourselves. Created beings cannot create, only imitate. Man can take things that have already been created and combine them to make something new. This is called being *creative*. Creativity is perhaps our most God-like quality, but it is not the same thing as speaking a word and seeing an entirely new form of creation appear.

When God created light, he simultaneously created darkness, or the opposite of light. If there is good, there is simultaneously the opposite. This creational relationship of opposites is demonstrated in Isaiah 45:7. I'm going to list several different translations of that Scripture to give you a feel of the different interpretations.

I form the light, and create darkness: I make peace, and create evil: I the LORD do all these things. (King James Version)

I form the light and create darkness, I bring prosperity and create disaster; I, the LORD, do all these things. (New International Version)

The One forming light and creating darkness, causing well-being and creating calamity; I am the LORD who does all these. (New American Standard)

I form light and create darkness, I make harmonies and create discords. I, God, do all these things. (The Message)

I form the light and create darkness, I make peace [national well-being] and I create [physical] evil (calamity); I am the Lord, Who does all these things. (Amplified)

Forming light, and preparing darkness, Making peace, and preparing evil, I am Jehovah, doing all these things. (Young's Literal Translation)

There are those that read this verse and see evil and chaos and destruction as coming from God. If God created good things, of course he automatically created evil things. Nothing can exist without its opposite (*or the possibility* of its nonexistence) existing. Because evil exists, it can be used by any created being. However, God does have the ability to work within and around every situation that exists. No matter what things are thrown at us, no matter what evil man can perpetrate against us; God can take the situation and use it to His glory. He can take the worst of the worst and turn it into something that ultimately becomes a blessing. There's the old adage "When life gives you lemons, make lemonade". When something that is not of God fills our life with lemons, God can easily hand us lemonade.

The Bible states clearly:

And we know that all things work together for good to them that love God, to them who are the called according to his purpose - Romans 8:28 (King James Version).

God is the creator of all things that exist. When God created understanding, he simultaneously created its opposite, which is *confusion*. Yet, in I Corinthians 14:33, it states that God is not the author of confusion. There is quite a difference in creating something, and in using or misusing that creation. Even though God created confusion, he doesn't use confusion to bring about his will. Therefore, when we see confusion manifest, we can be certain that the author is not God.

The same is true for hatred, or the opposite of love. God doesn't use hatred to achieve his will. However, when hatred is demonstrated, God has the ability to take that demonstration and turn it into a blessing. To illustrate this point, there was a man begging for food money at the side of the road, and a sympathetic passerby gave him $10. The beggar took the $10, bought a bottle of wine, and sat down by the road to drink it. Was the passerby in the wrong? After all, if he had never created the situation for the beggar to have money, the beggar wouldn't be drinking.

An hour later the passerby came through again and saw the beggar with the wine. Seeing the drunkard, he recognized himself from only a few years earlier. He stopped to share his story with the beggar, and in the course of events the beggar invited Christ into his life, gave up drinking, found a home off of the street, and began ministering to the homeless.

The passerby created a situation by giving the beggar money. Even though it was never the intention of the passerby, the money ended up being misused in a manner that was quite harmful to the beggar. The passerby didn't directly create a harmful situation, but once the situation had been created, the passerby was able to use the bad situation and turn it into something that was infinitely greater than supplying a beggar with $10 worth of food. God creates, man abuses or misuse, and then God takes that abuse and uses it to bring about His will.

Chapter 3
Out of control

As I stated in the introduction, you will find few (if any) examples in this book of my telling you what to think. Instead, this book is going to continually challenge you by making you think for yourself. By the time you're through with it, you'll not only possess the keys, but you'll have a good understanding of what I'm talking about when I say that it's time that we start learning *how* to think rather than *what* to think.

As a small example of what I'm talking about, let's say that you are a smoker. Someone might tell you that smoking cigarettes is wrong, and that Christians who smoke are committing a sin. Someone else might tell you that if you're committing sin, you will be punished for it. They can quote you scriptures about the body being the temple of the Lord, and then tell you that cigarette smoke destroys the temple. You might hear that if you are smoking, you are not only harming your body, but that you are destroying your Christian testimony, and perhaps causing others to stumble.

First of all, please understand that this is not about smoking. Personally, I don't smoke and I never have. In fact, I'm allergic to cigarette smoke and cannot be around it. The point that I'm making is that, whether they can actually back it up scripturally or not, there are people who will tell you that you are no longer allowed to smoke after becoming a Christian. The majority of Christians believe that a Christian should act a certain way, and should not act in other certain ways. There are people that believe you should do or not do certain things. You know that to be true, but have you ever thought why that is? Have you ever thought "Why does it matter to that person what I do?"

In the introduction to this book we talked about how from a very early age, we are told what to think. Why would that be? Why would somebody else want us to think a certain way? The answer is very simple... control. If your children think like you want them to think, they will be easier for you to control. If the classroom of students all think the same way, they are easier for the teacher to control. If the employees on the job think alike, they are easier to control. A good example of this can be seen watching a shepherd herd their sheep. The sheep all think alike. They are much easier to control, because the shepherd doesn't need to deal with each one of them individually. The shepherd controls the few sheep that are in front, and because all sheep think alike, they all follow and fall into place. How incredibly difficult a shepherd's job would be were each sheep to be an individual that thought for itself!

So, are we saying that control is a good thing? Well, of course control is a good thing. If you don't have control you have chaos. Get Smart. While the younger generation is Goggling the previous sentence, the rest of us can take time to ponder this issue of control. How far does the control go? Remember that it is ingrained in us from a very early age. We grow up in a culture of control, so it seems very natural to us. Does this control extend into our political choices? Without a doubt. How about church? Even more than you know. So, we are being controlled at church? Remember, that without control there is chaos. It would not be an enjoyable experience to attend a church where there is chaos.

There is no evil plan being perpetrated by your church. The pastor is not locked into some diabolical tryst with the Illuminati. The control at your church is subliminal and most likely at a completely unconscious level. Pastors are not trained to get their congregation all thinking alike, it is simply an outcropping of us growing up and living in an externally controlled environment. It's much like the way you learn to speak your native language. When did you learn to speak it? It's something that you can't put your finger on, because there was no particular time or event that occurred when you began learning to speak your native language. You simply grew up in the environment where it was spoken, and it just became natural to you. It became a part of who you are without your even realizing it. I heard Danny Silk use the *native language* analogy in his *Love*

Language seminars, and I thought it was brilliant. I simply had to use it here as it is so apropos to our discussion.

While most times not a conscious effort, or even operating from a level of consciousness; your church *does* need its congregation to think alike. If you don't think like everyone else, you might begin to ask questions. If your questions go unanswered, you might become restless and uneasy. If you become restless and uneasy at your church, you might start to visit other churches. If you find another church that seems to be able to answer your question, you might leave your church in favor of the new one. When you leave a church, your money goes with you. Pure and simple, it's about economics. Money is not evil, nor is the need of it (no matter how many times you've heard that misquoted from Scripture). The church needs your money in order to pay its overhead. As long as you are thinking like everyone else, you will stay, your money will stay, and the money will sustain the church.

It's calculated that 2 billion people (a third of the population of the world) profess to be Christian. It's also estimated that there are 30,000 Christian denominations or divisions in the world. On a sidebar, the conspiracy theorists might be interested to know the average number of people per denomination. It's simple math, 2 billion divided by 30,000. The answer is 66,666.666. Why has the Protestant church divided so many times? Because of control. If you don't think the same way that everyone else in your church thinks, then you cannot be controlled. If you cannot be controlled or if you cannot get in control of others, then our natural tendencies (the ones that we have grown up with... the ones that have been fostered throughout our childhood, school, job and social and political life) either tell us that you are not good for our congregation; or tell you that this congregation is not good for you.

Obviously, there needs to be control. The problem is that we have been raised to believe that that control has to be external. The only thing that we have ever known throughout our entire lives is that there has to be somebody else in control of us. Therein lays the problem. There has to be control, but we were not created and designed to be controlled externally. We were created and designed to be controlled internally. We refer to this as self-control. Because of this diametrical situation, we are always at odds with ourselves. Our intrinsically designed tendencies are to be self-controlled, but our natural-feeling, learned-response tendencies are to look for and accept external control.

Being internally controlled presents another problem. If we were to all use self control in the manner in which it was intended, it still wouldn't automatically have us all thinking alike. There are some whose self-control would never allow them to have an alcoholic drink. There are Christians who believe that it is okay to have a drink in the privacy of their own home, but would never do so in front of others. There are others whose self-control would allow them to enjoy a Dos Equis with their Mexican meal, and yet others who would be comfortable going on a cruise ship and having a few alcoholic drinks in the bar. If a new Christian convert wanted to present a proper Christian testimony, which one of the above scenarios would you instruct her to be the correct one?

If you realized that I asked a trick question, you are already well on your way of learning how to think rather than being told what to think. If you chose one of the scenarios to be the correct one, don't fret. You are thinking like the majority. Your answer is only a reflection of the culture in which we have been raised. Since I was partially raised the same way, I understand the thought process behind your answer (no matter which one you chose). So what's the correct answer? The above paragraph talks about having self-control. Self-control comes from within. If you were to choose the correct answer for the new convert, then you would be exhibiting external control. In other words, you would be telling her *what* to think, instead of *how* to think.

"But, she's a new convert!" You protest. "What if she chose the wrong thing to do? What if she drinks a beer in public and somebody sees her? I think that it's wrong to have a beer in public because you might offend people or send them the wrong message about how a Christian is supposed to act." If you find yourself thinking these things, just stop for a moment, take a deep breath and relax. I am not just writing those words for you to read over and then continue on in a frustrated state. **I'm very serious about this**. Put this book down. It won't go anywhere. It will be here when you come back. Lie back in a comfortable chair, close your eyes, breathe deeply and pray for guidance. If this is a new concept for you, let me give you the prayer to pray this time.

"Heavenly Father, I ask for your strength right now. I ask for your wisdom right now. I invite the Holy Spirit to show me and guide me into all truth. I don't want to be influenced by this writer if it is not of you. I don't want to simply be influenced to think the way that my boss, my spouse, my teacher or my pastor wants me to think. I only want to think and believe what you would have me think and believe. I ask the Holy Spirit to flood my entire being right now, and to give me His wisdom, understanding and guidance. I ask these things in Jesus' name. Amen."

Here's the situation. We are talking about the fact that we are created with a conscience, and the ability to be internally controlled; yet it's always in our learned nature to not only want to have external control, but to exert external control over others. I've read the entire Old Testament several times. I've read the entire New Testament many more times. I can say assuredly that this following verse is not to be found: "Thou shalt have no beer in public lest thou offendest the least of these." Through my attempt at humor, let me again remind you that this conversation is not about alcohol. I might have a beer once or twice a year with a meal, but for the most part I can say that I do not drink alcohol. I'm not defending it nor am I criticizing it because alcohol is not the issue. The issue is exerting control over someone else.

For far too long we have all been guilty of trying to exert external control over others. Unfortunately, this has long ago filtered into the church as well, to the point that it almost seems natural to debate Bible verses with Christians who don't understand them the same way that we do. It would seem unnatural if we didn't correct a new convert who has received a different understanding of a particular passage than that of our own. This is the beginning of the pathway to the keys, however. The pathway starts inside of us. If we don't get that part right, we will start down one of the thousands of wrong paths. Each of us needs to begin with ourselves. We need to learn how to rely on self-control. We need to learn our identity. We need to know the identity that has been stolen from us, and learn how to retrieve it.

We need to learn who God is. Not simply head-knowledge of the Creator who is sitting on the throne and watching over us; but we need to learn how to have a one-on-one relationship. It's time that we find out the truth about religion. It's time that we find out the truth about the message of Jesus. It's time that we hear His words, rather than the same old misinterpretations that we've always been told. It's time that we discover who we are. It's time that we discover our destiny. It's time that we rise up and change the world. It's time that we truly understand the meaning of the one and only prayer that Jesus taught us to pray. The keys have been stolen, and we have been locked outside for far too long.

As you might imagine, it's a long path to walk. I'm going to take you by the hand and walk with you. This book is our map. As you continue to read, you will not only eventually complete the path; but you will find the keys along the way. You will eventually unlock the door, enter in, and rush headlong into a world that you never knew existed. It's time that we open our eyes to the greatest paradigm shift since the crucifixion. Think of the scene in the Wizard of Oz when Dorothy first steps into Oz and everything turns into full-color. You are going to experience a much more dramatic entrance than that. But it all begins with baby steps

A Thin Place

God is always breaking into our natural world and showing us the spirit realm. A thin place is where our world and the realm of Heaven collide. It is easier to experience the spiritual realm in these places.

—Beni Johnson - from her book *The Happy Intercessor*

Where Heaven and Earth are close... that is so amazing! Sometimes we pass through these places unaware. We might get a chill and give a shiver, but keep on walking.

Sometimes we just need to stop and be silent and make ourselves aware of His presence. Sometimes we have to search the world to find such places, and sometimes it's in our back yard. I took this photo when I first got my camera. It was early autumn, my favorite time of the year. I went outside with the expectation that the Lord would show me something beautiful, and He allowed me see something that I have looked at a hundred times before, but never truly seen. I lifted my head to seek His face, opened my eyes and just at that moment... He came! I remember being so filled with joy and overcome with love, I almost forgot to raise my camera to snap the photo. To the untrained heart, this may just appear a picture of the sun behind a bush. To me, it's the Son coming through the branches... just to dance with me in the peaceful hour of the day.

—Lissa / Ironton, OH

This image may be freely downloaded for personal use at
ww.kingdomcultureministries.org

Chapter 4
How Can the Church Carry On?

"If it's true that the church is being held together by external control", you might ask "and you are suggesting that the control be eliminated, how will the church continued to exist?" That's a very good question, and I'm glad that you asked. To begin with, let's review the previous chapter. We read that mankind was designed to be self-controlled, but that man lived in continuous conflict because the self-control is continually usurped by various external controls. To begin walking down the path that leads to the Kingdom, we first must establish self-control, and eliminate external control. Of course, there are those external controls (such as from a teacher or boss) that will be much harder to completely eliminate, but the sooner that you learn that nobody on Earth can control you unless you allow them to, the better off you will be.

Without the external control of the church, or the congregation, or the teacher or preacher telling you what to think, you can start the process of thinking on your own. Once you come to your own conclusions, you may find those conclusions to be different from those of others in your church. Once you find that you have different understandings and beliefs than those of your fellow church members, it's time to leave to find another church... right? WRONG!

If you are Catholic, you most likely understand by now that most of the people in the church don't think exactly alike, but it's not a reason to leave the church. This part is not going to be as dramatic for you as it will be

27

for us Protestants. As some may be unfamiliar with the term 'Protestant', it refers to all of the churches stemming from the Reformation of the 16th century. As a basic rule of thumb, if you are a Christian and you are not Catholic, you're more than likely Protestant. The Protestants include all the well-known Christian denominations including: Baptists, Methodists, Lutheran, Apostolic, Anabaptists (such as the Amish), Brethren (such as the Mennonites) Pentecostals (such as Church of God, Assemblies of God) Charismatic (such as the Vineyard churches) Presbyterian, Reformed Churches, Church of Christ and the Latter Day Saints as well as many, many others and all of the thousands of different individual branches of the denominations listed here.

These, and all other Christian protestant churches, have their roots in the reformists that repudiated papal authority. The words *Protestant* and *protest* came about at the same time in Middle English, and were used to describe the people that were breaking away from the Catholic Church. They were not looked upon favorably, and the word *Protestant* was not considered a pleasant term. The protestors adopted it as their own moniker, however, and wore it proudly. This quick history lesson of the church was mainly presented in order to emphasize the word *protest* that was created at the time of the Reformation. People protested, and then left the church. That's how all of the denominations began, and so it's in both their heritage and in their gene pool. That's all they know.

As a result, for five hundred years they have continued in the manner in which they began. Whenever one or two or more disagree with a principle or interpretation, they protest. If the rest of the congregation does not see it their way, they are no longer able to fellowship with people who have a different belief, so they leave and start a different branch of the denomination, or an entirely new denomination. As an example, R.G. Spurling was a Baptist minister prior to the turn of the 20th century. He disagreed with some of the Baptist theology such as Landmarkism. Landmarkism is an ecclesiology which (very basically) states that only Baptists are true Christians. Spurlock started to be shunned by the Baptists around his home; so he and eight followers began the Christian Union. In 1903, a Quaker by the name of A. J. Tomlinson became the overseer of what was then being called The Church of God. Only a century later, there are perhaps a hundred different branches of the COG. The branch from Cleveland alone boasts approximately 5 million members in approximately twenty-seven thousand churches found in virtually every country on Earth.

While most past protestant church dissenters had the very best of intentions, it's time to stop. The fingers need to reattach to the hand, and the hand to the wrist. The time for division is no longer, and the hour of the church culture is passing away. The denominational differences are ending. It is ludicrous to still continue to think that we cannot be associated with someone who doesn't think exactly the way that we do. Do your spouse and you think exactly alike about every issue that you've ever discussed? How about your boyfriend or girlfriend? When you find out that they think differently than you do about some things, do you leave them? How about your job? Do you quit your job every time you disagree with the boss?

I'm sure that you'll find those questions ridiculous... but it's no less ridiculous to think that we have to believe exactly the way someone else believes to be able to go to worship with them. It's ingrained in us, and it needs to come out. Churches and pastors try to tell you what to think only as a basic survival strategy. They know that you will most likely leave if you don't think the same things that they do.

So step number one on the journey down the pathway is to decide to become self-controlled, rather than being controlled by those around you. There's going to be a lot more happening inside you as you continue down the pathway to the ultimate you, but those things will come as they come. For now, remember... baby steps. Once you decide that you are going to start thinking for yourself, you are going to find that you no longer think like those around you. A sheep has broken away from the herd! You can stay with the herd, however. You don't have to leave your church just because you start discovering new truths.

When most people start to realize that the path they have been on is never going to take them where they want to go, they want to tell others about it as well. Keep in mind that others are not going to be quite so receptive to all of your new revelations if you spring it on them all at once. The revelations have not even been shown to you at this time. They're going to come very slowly as you continue to read so that you won't be overwhelmed. If you are hungry for God, you're going to find them refreshing. Not everyone has your hunger. Perhaps a better introduction for them would be to share this book once you're finished.

Keep in mind that it's time to start acting like big boys and girls. If they don't see things your way, it's no longer considered appropriate to run off to find someone else to play with. On the other hand, Kingdom revelations are being given to people all across the world. There are incredible bodies of believers in all 50 states of the United States and in virtually every country in the world that have the same revelations that you'll be getting. There are ways to find them, if you are interested, that we will discuss later. Always keep in mind, however, that you never want to seek out any different fellowship of believers simply in order to find someone else who believes like you do. The only reason to move to another church or fellowship is for you to grow and learn more about the Kingdom of God, or when God directs you to do so.

How will churches carry on? They will carry on as more and more of their congregation comes to the realization that we all don't have to think exactly alike to be able to fellowship together. Some people leave church after church after church trying to find the perfect one that believes exactly the way they do. That's not how we are supposed to live. We who are called by His name are supposed to fellowship together. Jesus' own disciples didn't see eye to eye on most things, but they shared a common love of Jesus.

That's how we are to live. The first thing that comes out of a Christian's mouth when meeting another Christian is "Where do you go to church?" or "What denomination are you?" That's a very sad commentary on what we've become, because what we're actually saying is: "Tell me what you believe so that I can decide whether we should be talking." This needs to end. It's time for the fingernail to realize that it's useless without the finger. It's time for the finger to realize that it's useless without the knuckle.... Get my drift?

Chapter 5
Two Billion Christians Can't Be Wrong

Could there be things that Christians have always been told and hold to be true, that just simply aren't scriptural? Think back to the section entitled how to read this book. Remember some of the things that were mentioned? Remember that Edison didn't invent the light bulb? Napoleon wasn't short and turkey doesn't make you sleepy. Were there any of those things that you have always believed? Bear with me for a moment, and let's revisit the very first sentence and paragraph of the introduction to this book. Have you ever been wrong about anything? How about a relationship? How about a love interest? Have you ever been in a relationship that you believed to be true, only to be hurt or to find out that you had been lied to? How passionately did you love? How deeply did you believe in the relationship, only to find out later that it was a lie?

It's time to make a decision. Now is the time, this is the place... right here right now, right where you are. *As God's fellow workers we urge you not to receive God's grace in vain. For he says, "In the time of my favor I heard you, and in the day of salvation I helped you. I tell you, now is the time of God's favor, now is the day of salvation* - II Corinthians 6:1-2 (New International Version). You might have been told that this scripture is only for a witnessing tool to the lost, however all scripture is alive in the fact that it tends to change, grow and mold to our needs each time we read. Many times, verses that you have never paid attention to before will suddenly jump out and speak to you. Might this verse be telling you that today is the day that everything changes in your walk with the Lord?

At this point in the book, you have a couple of choices. You can choose to continue on with your Christian walk just as you have been living it; if you're happy with the results that it has been producing. You can continue going to church or not going to church, and doing the same things from now on that you have always done...and you will continue to see the same results. Or you can say "There has to be something more". Are you totally satisfied and completely happy with every aspect of your walk; and with the fruit that you see it yielding? Most likely the answer is "no" or you wouldn't be reading this book.

If you choose to continue reading, you might just discover that the Christian life is nothing like what you have always been taught. In fact, you might find it the extreme opposite. It's much bigger, it's much more exciting, it's much more fun, and it's much more free, powerful, entertaining and exhilarating. There are a lot of things to come and a lot of truths to be opened up, as well as some strongholds that may need to fall, so brace yourself, and hold on... we're heading into the rapids!

Before you read any further, I would ask you one more time to pray the prayer that you prayed in Chapter 3. Don't just read over these words; pray this prayer from your heart. The scripture says that *when the Spirit of Truth comes, he will guide you into all truth. He will not speak on his own accord, but will speak whatever he hears and will declare to you the things that are to come* - John 16:13 (New International Version)

"Heavenly Father, I ask for your strength right now. I ask for your wisdom right now. I invite the Holy Spirit to show me and guide me into all truth. I don't want to be influenced by this writer if it is not of you. I don't want to simply be influenced to think the way that my boss, my spouse, my teacher or my pastor wants me to think. I only want to think and believe what you would have me think and believe. I ask the Holy Spirit to flood my entire being right now, and to give me His wisdom, understanding and guidance. I ask these things in Jesus' name. Amen."

This is a good prayer to commit to memory, or at least commit the gist of the prayer to memory. The biggest reason for there being so many wrong interpretations of Scripture is that there are many people who read it, to whom it was not written. Many people read the Bible with their mind only, and not with the spirit. As you continually pray for the guidance of the Holy Spirit, you are going to see some incredible things happen. You are going to read things that you have never heard before, and possibly read things that are the exact opposite of everything that you've ever been told... and even though your mind might initially hesitate, the spirit in you will bear witness and leap for joy. Even before you completely understand it in your mind, your spirit will be screaming yes! "Yes! Yes! This is truth! This is the *something more* that I've always been looking for!"

In order to learn *how* to think about God and *how* to think about the Bible, rather than being told *what* to think, you need to lay aside most everything that you've ever learned about *what* the Bible says... and learn *how* God wants to communicate with you. Notice that I didn't say lay aside the Bible, nor did I say lay aside Bible verses. Please don't misunderstand. *All scripture is given by inspiration of God, and is profitable for doctrine, for reproof, for correction, for instruction in righteousness* - **II** Timothy 3:16 (King James Version). What we need to lay aside is man's interpretation of the Bible. Unfortunately, for most of us, we have gone to church, listened to preachers, talked to other Christians, read books and listened to radio, TV and other recorded sermons for so long that sometimes the line becomes blurred. Sometimes we truly can't decipher what we've actually read in the scriptures, and what we were told was in the scriptures. Believe me, it's usually not one and the same thing.

How many times have you heard someone misquote Paul's letter to Timothy as having stated: "money is the root of all evil"? While those exact words can be seen in the text, people do not quote the entire scripture. The verse actually reads: *For the love of money is the root of all evil: which while some coveted after, they have erred from the faith, and pierced themselves through with many sorrows* - I Timothy 6:10 (King James Version). In reading the entire verse, it's now plain to see that Paul was not speaking about money, he was speaking about the love or lust for the things of this world. To *lust* after money is the root of all evil. In other words, it's not the money itself that's evil, it's the greed. My interpretation would be something of this order: Evil thoughts begin when someone starts lusting after the things of this world.

In the next chapter we will begin exploring the scripture to learn the truths that have been hidden there. Why would God hide things from us you might ask? God doesn't hide things from us, he hides things *for* us. The scriptures that we are going to be reading are going to jump out at you plain as day, and you will be asking yourself over and over "why have

I never read this before?" Of course, you know that you've read it many times, and possibly for many years; but even when it is right in front of our faces, God can keep it hidden. It has been hidden away for us for such a time as this. It is God's timetable.

"So why am I not hearing this in my church?" You might ask. "Why hasn't my pastor preached on these things?" First of all, I always like to address the alarmists before the seeds can be planted. There is no conspiracy. Your church is not in league with some world council of churches that is secretly planning the overthrow of Christianity. The truth is nothing more than the fact that God is just now starting to reveal His plan. You might start seeing some of it fall into place before your pastor does. This is God's timetable, and we have to respect the fact that He's in charge, and He knows what He's doing.

The reason that God's word is coming alive to us, and He's just now showing us his plan is that we now find ourselves at the beginning of a paradigm shift. The church has been divided for too long. This was never God's intention. God doesn't want us to be caught up in denominationalism. His Word teaches us just the opposite. He wants us to draw together, to become one body, to present ourselves unblemished as a bride awaiting a bridegroom.

I want you to think about how all this makes you more significant, not less. A body isn't just a single part blown up into something huge. It's all the different-but-similar parts arranged and functioning together. If Foot said, "I'm not elegant like Hand, embellished with rings; I guess I don't belong to this body," would that make it so? If Ear said, "I'm not beautiful like Eye, limpid and expressive; I don't deserve a place on the head," would you want to remove it from the body? If the body was all eye, how could it hear? If all ear, how could it smell? As it is, we see that God has carefully placed each part of the body right where he wanted it.

But I also want you to think about how this keeps your significance from getting blown up into self-importance. For no matter how significant you are, it is only because of what you are a part of. An enormous eye or a gigantic hand wouldn't be a body, but a monster. What we have is one body with many parts, each its proper size and in its proper place. No part is important on its own. Can you imagine Eye telling Hand, "Get lost; I don't need you"? Or, Head telling Foot, "You're fired; your job has been phased out"? As a matter of fact, in practice it works the other way—the "lower" the part, the more basic, and therefore necessary. You can live without an eye, for instance, but not without a stomach. When it's a part of your own body you are concerned with, it makes no difference whether the part is visible or clothed, higher or lower. You give it dignity and honor just as it is, without comparisons. If anything, you have more concern for the lower parts than the higher. If you had to choose, wouldn't you prefer good digestion to full-bodied hair?

The way God designed our bodies is a model for understanding our lives together as a church: every part dependent on every other part, the parts we mention and the parts we don't, the parts we see and the parts we don't. If one part hurts, every other part is involved in the hurt, and in the healing. If one part flourishes, every other part enters into the exuberance.

You are Christ's body—that's who you are! You must never forget this. Only as you accept your part of that body does your "part" mean anything. You're familiar with some of the parts that God has formed in his church, which is his "body" - I Corinthians 12:14-30 (The Message).

Most times we are just too caught up in the programs, ministries, events and trappings of denominationalism to see what God is trying to do. Keep in mind that it's not the name on the door of your church that creates a division. It's not the denomination or the branch of the denomination that you attend that separates us... it's the heart. If you have a heart after the denomination, then division is what you will receive. If you have a heart that is seeking after the heart of God, then you will find it.

"Don't bargain with God. Be direct. Ask for what you need. This isn't a cat-and-mouse, hide-and-seek game we're in. If your child asks for bread, do you trick him with sawdust? If he asks for fish, do you scare him with a live snake on his plate? As bad as you are, you wouldn't think of such a thing. You're at least decent to your own children. So don't you think the God who conceived you in love will be even better?" - Matthew 7:7-11 (The Message).

Religion teaches us what to think. The goal of any type of "Christian" religious teaching is to persuade us that it is correct. Denominationalism supports the idea that when people tell us what to think and we agree with them; then we can fellowship together. The more people that agree, the bigger the church attendance can grow. The bigger the attendance grows the more money that the business of religion can generate. The flipside of that belief however, is the reason that the protestant churches have split over thirty thousand times since their inception a few hundred years ago. If we agree with each other, we stay together. If we don't agree, someone will leave and start another split.

Once a Christian discovers how that God designed him to think for himself, he can no longer be controlled by the rules of religion. Without rules, there can be no control. Without control over its members, religious organizations have no way to sustain themselves. Their only means of retaliation against the breaking down of their strongholds of control is to; once again, tell their members **what** to think. In the next chapter we are going to learn Jesus' teachings about the Kingdom. Even though it will be word for word directly from the Scripture, the religious will brand Kingdom teaching as "cultish" or even as heresy. This is usually strong enough language to control the congregation, and persuade them to follow the rules and not study it for themselves. After all, who wants to be branded a cult?

So that we can all remain on the same page, I want to include the meanings that I put behind the terms church and religion. Unless otherwise noted, I use the term *church* to refer to the buildings built by the various denominations, as well as the people that attend that building who are truly seeking the heart of God. As far as the term religion and religious goes, I use those terms when referring to people who go to church for show, social status, or social gathering, while never experiencing God's will for their life. These people are usually set in their ways and have little interest in seeking the face of the Lord to learn what He would have them to do. I make no judgment call on them whatsoever; I just have a term that I refer to them by... religious.

The religious are no different today than they were in the days of Christ walking the Earth. Things change. The times change. Seasons change both in the physical and in the spiritual. Ways of doing things and of getting things accomplished change. Technology changes. People don't change. The Word of God is many things. There are believers who refer to the Bible as the Word of God, and believe it to be the cure all and end all of God's dealings with man. That way of thinking is purely a creation. It's a lie from the enemy to steal away our identity, and leave us powerless. If you want to know what the Word of God truly encompasses, then all you need to do is look to the scripture. However, the Bible is the most misused, misquoted, misunderstood writing in all of creation. The reason is that it was not simply written out of the mind of man; but from the mind of God.

The mind of man cannot even fathom the totality of the existence of an omnipotent (all powerful) omnipresent (being in every place at the same time) being, much less understand the thinking of such a being.

"For my thoughts are not your thoughts, neither are your ways my ways," declares the LORD. *"As the heavens are higher than the earth, so are my ways higher than your ways and my thoughts than your thoughts."* Isaiah 55:8-9 (New International Version).

When people say that God doesn't work in a certain way, or doesn't communicate in a certain way, or doesn't do this or do that... they are limiting God to their own understanding. Their God is no bigger than they are. Think about this: If something can be accomplished by human knowledge or abilities, be it Church service, feeding the poor, curing sickness, sheltering the homeless, or any other good work; then what part do we really need God for?

Repurposed

Seek the ingredients and steps for creating a culture around you that hosts the presence of God.

—Danny silk - from the book *Culture of Honor*

I love finding meaning in my photos. I always ask "What do they say to me?", and "What do they say through me?"

This photo is of an old train bridge that was renovated into a road for motor vehicle travel. I love the fact that it was originally intended for one purpose, but as the needs of the road changed, it's purpose and accessibility options changed as well. This reminds me of the story from Matthew when the gentile woman went to Jesus pleading for healing for her daughter. Jesus initially responded that He was there for an intended purpose, but as the woman's faith was strong, Jesus saw a different purpose to meet her need.

And, behold, a woman of Canaan came out of the same coasts, and cried unto him, saying, Have mercy on me, O Lord, thou son of David; my daughter is grievously vexed with a devil. But he answered her not a word. And his disciples came and besought him, saying, Send her away; for she crieth after us. But he answered and said, I am not sent but unto the lost sheep of the house of Israel. Then came she and worshipped him, saying, Lord, help me. But he answered and said, It is not meet to take the children's bread, and to cast it to dogs. And she said, Truth, Lord: yet the dogs eat of the crumbs which fall from their masters' table. Then Jesus answered and said unto her, O woman, great is thy faith: be it unto thee even as thou wilt. And her daughter was made whole from that very hour.

Matthew 15:22-28 (King James Version)

His accessibility changed. He came for one purpose, but in the right time, changed it for another. This woman honored the Lord Jesus. She exalted Him even when being compared to dogs. They tried to send her away, but she was setting up something far too great to be dismissed. She was cultivating an environment to host the Lord's presence. With her words and actions, she laid out a spread that invited Jesus to come in. Yes, she was from the "wrong side of the tracks" so to speak, but even she knew how access the Lord. It is my prayer that we each go to Him as we have need, regardless of the condition we are in. Even if the world says to you that you cannot be helped, and that the Kingdom of Heaven is not for your kind, I want you to understand that you can still go to Him. If need be, He will change His accessibility just for that one hungry heart. You can go broken and bitter, and full of sin and shame. You can go confused and angry and tormented. Just go. He died for you, just the way you are right now, so listening to you isn't an inconvenience for Him. He loves you. Jesus was the originator of "lay it on me."

In the same manner that He will accept you as you are, I would pray for you to accept others. Don't judge or condemn, just love as Jesus loves.

For God so loved the world, that he gave his only begotten Son, that whosoever believeth in him should not perish, but have everlasting life. For God sent not his Son into the world to condemn the world; but that the world through him might be saved.

John 3:16-17 (King James Version)

—Lissa / Hitchens, KY

This image may be freely downloaded for personal use at www.kingdomcultureministries.org

Chapter 6
Enter the Kingdom

"I've heard a lot about this kingdom stuff... so what is it anyway? Is this some type of cult? Why do we need these new teachings when we already have the Bible?" Well, hello to you too, and welcome to chapter 6. If you've made it this far, then you're obviously seeking. *Ask, and it shall be given you; seek, and ye shall find; knock, and it shall be opened unto you* - Matthew 7:7 (King James Version). We will be addressing these questions and others, but let's start with a dose of reality.

If you get your answers from the mind of man, then your answers will always be suspect. The next person that you hear from with a different take and a convincing argument could win you over just as easily. While there's nothing wrong with my simply telling you the answers, you don't truly know me. Though I will do my best to display it within the pages of this book, at this time you don't truly know where my heart is. There is nothing wrong with listening to your pastor, as long as you know him and know where his heart is. Keep in mind however, that pastors are only human. They make mistakes as well.

When you are seeking an answer from God, it's always best to go to the source. For many, this can be a foreign concept. Let's begin with the most important means in which you may communicate with God. I'm sure that many will automatically assume that it is prayer... but it's not. By far, the method of communication with God that takes priority is worship. Psalm 22:3 tells us that God inhabits (or lives or dwells in) the praises of his people. Jesus leaves little doubt that He will be in the midst of worshipers when he states *"For where two or three are gathered together in my name, there am I in the midst of them"* - Matthew 18:20 (King James Version). If you want to see and know God, you have to praise Him. The 16th chapter of Acts relays the happenings of Paul and Silas being thrown into prison. Around midnight, they began praising God, and at that moment, an Earthquake shook the foundations of the prison, and all at once all the prison doors flew open, and everybody's chains came loose. This is the power that is set into motion when we praise!

Is God so egocentric that He requires our constant praise? Of course not. God is complete within Himself, and in need of nothing from any outside source, much less from humanity. So why does He ask us to praise? Praise is a gift, but we have misunderstood it as a gift that we give to God. In actuality, it is a gift that God gives to us. God does not ask us to praise Him in order that He can receive something from us, but that we may receive something from Him. When we praise God, He will be right there in our midst. What better time to access Him than when He is with us? Few understand how important praise and worship is in the Kingdom of God.

Prayer is asking or telling God something. There will come a time when there is no longer a need for it. Bible verses are for our edification while on Earth. The Earth will eventually be destroyed, and along with it, every Bible. There will be no need for Bibles once we are in perfect relationship with the Creator, as His word will be in our hearts. The religious community has always erroneously put the emphasis of church service on preaching, with worship being only an opening act. However, there will come a time when preaching and preachers are no longer needed. There will never come a time when we will no longer praise and worship.

If we desire to know God's Heart, we must learn how to praise and worship. Understand that while we are alive here on Earth, we are training to be what we are ultimately created to be in the Kingdom. If we don't strive to get it right here on Earth, there won't be a magical transformation that will make us the greatest in the Kingdom once we die. As a matter of fact, if we don't develop the Kingdom lifestyle here, even what little we have been given will be stripped from us. That's what Jesus was trying to teach us in the parable of the talents recorded in Matthew 25:14-30 and Luke 19:12-28.

Something to understand is that praise does not simply consist of singing. Of course you can raise your arms, lift your head, close your eyes and sing out in joy to the one who has given you life, and He will dwell among those praises. But praise consists of many things. You can praise simply by standing still in the glory of His presence, and absorbing. You can praise by opening your mouth and your heart in speaking to Him, even when you might not understand exactly what you're saying... but you know it is praise. You can praise God by giving a tithe (or 10% of your income) to the church or ministry. Once again, God doesn't need your money. He's not asking for money from you, He's asking to be able to bless your life and show Himself to you through your obedience and praise. You can give God praise simply by walking in His pure, unadulterated love; and allowing others to see God in you. In praising God, we are inviting Him into our realm. Once He is in our midst, we can start to see the Kingdom of Heaven breakthrough into the Earth.

When you're not used to taking everything to the Lord in prayer and seeing the answers revealed, it can be a bit daunting when someone tells you to pray for the answer. We'll discuss more about prayer and how to use it later in the book; but another great method to learn the mind of God is in reading the Bible. Once again though, there is a catch. Not just anyone can open up the Bible and read it and understand what it is saying. Without prayer for guidance, wisdom and understanding, and without a pure heart truly seeking the face of God, one will leave empty-handed; or worse yet with a completely misconstrued or misunderstood way of thinking.

I want to begin with an easy concept that's a little more black and white than some, and a little easier to understand in the scripture than some. Still, continually pray for the guidance of the Holy Spirit. What I've decided to do is to simply provide short answer to the questions that you might be wondering about, then list the scripture that references the answers, and finally, to discuss in greater detail the answers as they relate to the scripture. So, to short answer the questions in order: What is Kingdom teaching? Kingdom teaching is a continuance of Christ's teachings. This is not a continuance as in an "addition to", I'm using the word simply to denote that we are to continue repeating the Kingdom message that Christ began.

Is it a cult? It is not. Of course, any ball team, fraternal, church or hobby enthusiast might be labeled as a cult by some, as it's a subjective thing.

What is your definition of a cult? I can tell you that I'm intensely devoted to my Lord and Savior. Below is an exact copy and paste from Merriam-Webster online dictionary:

Entry Word: **cult** Function: *noun*

Meaning: **1** a group of people showing intense devotion to a cause, person, or work.

Seems to me like a trick question. Though if it would make you feel better to read the words in print, the Kingdom message is not a cult; it is a movement of Christians to get back to the heart of God and the teachings of Christ, and away from man-made doctrine.

As to why a new teaching when we already have the Bible, this answer is going to perhaps be the most difficult for some. I wrote quite a bit about myths that we believe to be true in the *How to Read This Book* section. One of the reasons for that was to prepare you for this paragraph. The truth is, Kingdom teaching is what Jesus' life was all about. It's what the New Testament is all about. But instead of being taught that, we have been taught that we need to be in church, that we need to invite other people to church and that we should tell sinners that they are hell-bound and need to change their ways before it is too late. My question to you would be "Where is any of this found in the Bible?" If we are supposed to invite people to come to church with us so that they might get saved, why doesn't the Bible at least allude to that somewhere? 'Teaching about the Kingdom' is not new stuff... it's exactly what Jesus did. To start with, I just want to list some of the Scriptures that back this up. In subsequent chapters we will go into detail about what it all means.

The ministry of Jesus is recorded throughout the Gospels. Starting with the first gospel, which is Matthew, the ministry of Jesus can be traced from beginning to end. When Jesus first started to preach, His message was about the Kingdom. *From that time Jesus began to preach and to say, "Repent, for the kingdom of Heaven is at hand."* - Matthew 4:17 (King James Version).

After the Gospels comes the book of Acts. This book records the events after Jesus' death. After His death, He appeared to His disciples for a period of 40 days in order that all would have irrefutable proof of His resurrection. These 40 days after His death were His last days on Earth.

What was most on His mind during those days? What things did He talk about?

...of all that Jesus began both to do and teach, until the day in which he was taken up, after that he through the Holy Ghost had given commandments unto the apostles whom he had chosen: To whom also he shewed himself alive after his passion by many infallible proofs, being seen of them forty days, and speaking of the things pertaining to the kingdom of God - Acts 1:1 – 3 (King James Version).

So, the very first thing that Jesus started to preach about was the Kingdom. After His death and resurrection, the very last things that He taught about before He ascended into Heaven was the Kingdom. If those were all of the references in regards to the Kingdom, we would have to conclude that teaching about the Kingdom was of immeasurable importance to Jesus. But this is far from all. As a matter of fact, we've not yet begun to scratch the surface.

The only recorded time that Jesus taught us how to pray by giving us the words, they were these: *Thy kingdom come, Thy will be done in Earth, as it is in Heaven* - Matthew 6:10 (King James Version). How important was this Kingdom message to Jesus? Here are a few more excerpts of Jesus' ministry throughout the book of Matthew. All of these verses are quoted from the King James Version of the Bible:

Matthew 4:23 *And Jesus went about all Galilee, teaching in their synagogues, and preaching the gospel of the kingdom, and healing all manner of sickness and all manner of disease among the people.*

Matthew 5:3 *Blessed are the poor in spirit: for theirs is the kingdom of Heaven.*

Matthew 5:10 *Blessed are they which are persecuted for righteousness' sake: for theirs is the kingdom of Heaven.*

Matthew 5:9-11*Whosoever therefore shall break one of these least commandments, and shall teach men so, he shall be called the least in the kingdom of Heaven: but whosoever shall do and teach them, the same shall be called great in the kingdom of Heaven.*

On the extremely rare occasion in which Jesus spoke negatively, He reserved that negativity for the church. The church of that day was much like many churches of this day. People went to church just to be seen. It had become a social gathering place. Most of the members were not interested in righteousness, but in having their good deeds seen and praised by men. The most religious men in the church in those days, the senior pastors and TV evangelists of their day, were called the Pharisees. Of course, there are many Godly TV evangelists and senior pastors today; but Jesus is speaking to the self-righteous and the hypocrites. About them, Jesus said:

For I say unto you, that except your righteousness shall exceed the righteousness of the scribes and Pharisees, ye shall in no case enter into the kingdom of Heaven. (Matthew 5:20)

Matthew 6:13 Jesus prayed: *For thine is the kingdom, and the power, and the glory, forever.*

Matthew 6:33 *But seek ye first the kingdom of God, and his righteousness; and all these things shall be added unto you.*

Matthew 7:21 Not *everyone that saith unto me, Lord, Lord, shall enter into the kingdom of Heaven; but he that doeth the will of my Father which is in Heaven.*

Matthew 8:11 *And I say unto you, that many shall come from the east and west, and shall sit down with Abraham, and Isaac, and Jacob, in the kingdom of Heaven.*

Matthew 9:35 *And Jesus went about all the cities and villages, teaching in their synagogues, and preaching the gospel of the kingdom, and healing every sickness and every disease among the people.*

Matthew 10:7 *And as ye go, preach, saying, the kingdom of Heaven is at hand.*

Matthew 11:11 *Verily I say unto you, Among them that are born of women there hath not risen a greater than John the Baptist: notwithstanding he that is least in the kingdom of Heaven is greater than he.*

Matthew 11:12 *And from the days of John the Baptist until now the kingdom of Heaven suffereth violence, and the violent take it by force.*

Matthew 12:28 *But if I cast out devils by the Spirit of God, then the kingdom of God is come unto you.*

Matthew 13:11 *He answered and said unto them, because it is given unto you to know the mysteries of the kingdom of Heaven, but to them it is not given.*

Matthew 13:19 *When any one heareth the word of the kingdom, and understandeth it not, then cometh the wicked one, and catcheth away that which was sown in his heart.*

Matthew 13:24 *Another parable put he forth unto them, saying, The kingdom of Heaven is likened unto a man which sowed good seed in his field:*

Matthew 13:31 *Another parable put he forth unto them, saying, The kingdom of Heaven is like to a grain of mustard seed, which a man took, and sowed in his field:*

Matthew 13:33 *Another parable spake he unto them; The kingdom of Heaven is like unto leaven, which a woman took, and hid in three measures of meal, till the whole was leavened.*

Matthew 13:38 *The field is the world; the good seed are the children of the kingdom; but the tares are the children of the wicked one;*

Matthew 13:41 *The Son of man shall send forth his angels, and they shall gather out of his kingdom all things that offend, and them which do iniquity;*

Matthew 13:43 Then shall the righteous shine forth as the sun in the kingdom of their Father. Matthew 13:44 *Again, the kingdom of Heaven is like unto treasure hid in a field; the which when a man hath found, he hideth, and for joy thereof goeth and selleth all that he hath, and buyeth that field.*

Matthew 13:45 *the kingdom of Heaven is like unto a merchant man, seeking goodly pearls:*

Matthew 13:47 *the kingdom of Heaven is like unto a net, that was cast into the sea, and gathered of every kind:*

Matthew 13:52 *Then said he unto them, Therefore every scribe which is instructed unto the kingdom of Heaven is like unto a man that is an householder, which bringeth forth out of his treasure things new and old.*

Matthew 16:19 *And I will give unto thee the keys of the kingdom of Heaven: and whatsoever thou shalt bind on Earth shall be bound in Heaven: and whatsoever thou shalt loose on Earth shall be loosed in Heaven.*

Matthew 16:28 *Verily I say unto you, There be some standing here, which shall not taste of death, till they see the Son of man coming in his kingdom.*

Matthew 18:1 At the same time came the disciples unto Jesus, saying, Who is the greatest in the kingdom of Heaven?

Matthew 18:3 *And said, Verily I say unto you, Except ye be converted, and become as little children, ye shall not enter into the kingdom of Heaven.*

Matthew 18:4 *Whosoever therefore shall humble himself as this little child, the same is greatest in the kingdom of Heaven.*

Matthew 18:23 *Therefore is the kingdom of Heaven likened unto a certain king, which would take account of his servants.*

Matthew 19:14 *But Jesus said, Suffer little children, and forbid them not, to come unto me: for of such is the kingdom of Heaven.*

Matthew 19:23 *Then said Jesus unto his disciples, Verily I say unto you, that a rich man shall hardly enter into the kingdom of Heaven.*

Matthew 19:24 *And again I say unto you, It is easier for a camel to go through the eye of a needle, than for a rich man to enter into the kingdom of God.*

Matthew 20:1 *For the kingdom of Heaven is like unto a man that is an householder, which went out early in the morning to hire labourers into his vineyard.*

Matthew 21:31 *Jesus saith unto them, Verily I say unto you, that the publicans and the harlots go into the kingdom of God before you.* (In speaking to the religious)

Matthew 21:43 *Therefore say I unto you, The kingdom of God shall be taken from you, and given to a nation bringing forth the fruits thereof.*

Matthew 22:2-3 *The kingdom of Heaven is like unto a certain king, which made a marriage for his son, and sent forth his servants to call them that were bidden to the wedding: and they would not come.*

How sad that Jesus Himself brought the Kingdom message, and many rejected it. From the creation of Adam and Eve to this very day, God has only wanted a relationship with us. He wants to establish a Kingdom in which to be able to fellowship with us, but we keep rejecting it. The denominationalism and division of the body of Christ that has existed in the world for the past five centuries are not of God's doing, but of man's. Even though God has tolerated the division... and even blessed people who continued to seek Him in spite of it, it has never been His way. Now things are changing. Look around the world at what is beginning to happen to the true church. We are entering into a new time, a new dispensation, a new move of God. God is preparing His bride for the relationship that He has always longed for.

There are other Kingdom references in the book of Matthew, and there are many more throughout the remaining gospels, not to mention throughout the rest of the entire New Testament. I have compiled some of them, and they can be read along with my commentary on them in addendum 1, at the back of this book. Also, following along with the Kingdom messages of Jesus through the book of Matthew, one comes to chapter 23 where Kingdom references are used in His scathing remarks about organized religion. I have presented those comments in addendum 2. Even though the content of the two addenda would fall within the next two chapters chronologically, they did not flow well in the scheme of the book, and were not conducive to the thought processes that we are establishing. I would most highly recommend you to continue to follow along with the chapters in order, and read the addenda later.

Chapter 7
The Big Scary God

In the previous chapter, we have well-established that the ministry of Jesus consisted of kingdom teaching. Exactly what does that Kingdom teaching consists of, though? I thoroughly cover that in the upcoming chapters of the book, but there are a couple of things more important to establish before we get to that. Kingdom teaching is all about relationships. It's about the relationships that you have with your friends, family, church, coworkers and social acquaintances; but most importantly it's about the relationship you have with God.

As with any relationship between any two entities, before we can talk about the intricacies and logistics of the relationship; we must know who is involved in the relationship. We are talking about a relationship between you and God, but who are you... and who is God? These are important questions to answer, because who you are and what you are; as well as what and who God is play an all-important role in how the relationship can be established and maintained. We will discuss *you* in the next chapter. In this chapter we are going to concentrate on who God is.

The title of this chapter, *The Big Scary God*, was chosen for good reason. The reason is that this is exactly how a good portion of the world views God. We constantly hear about the wrath of God. Whether nature produces floods, tornadoes, lightning strikes, hailstorms, tsunamis, or any other number of naturally occurring calamities; they are referred to in the media (and most likely by your insurance company) as *Acts of God*. God must be awfully mean, or at least terribly vengeful, to visit all of those devastating forces upon defenseless mankind. No doubt you've heard about the *Day of Judgment* when we must stand before God so that He might determine our eternal destiny. Scary! Have you read about God destroying the entire population of the world (other than Noah and his family, who escaped on the Ark)? What about Sodom and Gomorrah? In the Old Testament, God called for the destruction of many an enemy of Israel. He didn't spare women or children or sometimes even the animals that belonged to those he named as an enemy.

God seemed to have a bloodlust as well. To make a covenant in the Old Testament, participants were required to cut an animal in half, and each of them were required to walk through the gore. In order to obtain forgiveness for wrongdoing, the Jewish people were required to sacrifice animals to God upon an altar. When it came time for the ultimate sacrifice for the redemption of mankind, God sent His son to be humiliated, tortured and murdered. Now tell me that that doesn't sound like a big scary God!

Allow me to offer some insight about this subject in the form of a parable. Let's say that there was a horrendous crime committed against your family. Let's say that your young school aged daughter was tortured and raped, and you are now sitting in the courtroom at the trial of the man who has openly admitted to committing the crime. You can see the judge's face beginning to turn crimson in anger as the non-repentant criminal's carefree manner tries to make a mockery of the court. You watch the judge's teeth clench and lips thin as he stares coldly at the person who has nonchalantly ripped your heart out, destroyed your daughter's innocence, and decimated your family. The judge is so infuriated by this callous act that he can barely control his hands from shaking. As he is ready to issue his sentence and delve out the punishment of the court, it occurs to you that this judge is all powerful. He is almighty within the confines of his courtroom. He controls the power of life and death. My question to you is... are you afraid of him?

Are you afraid that the judge might issue too severe a punishment to the criminal? Are you scared of what might be running through his mind? Are you terrified at the thought of hearing his mighty voice ring out in the courtroom in order to demand justice? "These questions are ludicrous", you will surely reply "How could I, and why *would* I be afraid of someone who is about to deliver me justice?" you query. Why would you be scared?

Because he is almighty, because in him is all power and authority, because in his hands he holds the power of life and death.

Even though you don't see him in that light, there are many that fear this judge. They fear him for the same reasons that you now take comfort in. They fear him because in his hands lie the power of life and death for them. He has the ability to give them a second chance, or to lock them away from their friends and family. It's all a matter of perspective. Whether you fear him, or put your hope for justice in him depends on the relationship that you have with the judge. It depends on what side of the law you find yourself.

Let's continue on with our story. The perpetrator who violated your young daughter has a bit of a smirk on his face. He turns around and looks at you and your wife, and winks and blows a kiss at her. Your face flushes and your blood boils as you start to jump to your feet to lunge towards this animal. Your wife grabs your shirt and holds on as you start coming to your senses and realize where you are. You sit down in your seat and await the verdict that will allow you to start the healing process. The judge's face is set like stone. His stare could burn a hole clear through the child rapist.

You slide to the edge of your seat and your heart begins to race as the judge opens his mouth. "For this heartless, despicable crime... you *deserve* to be tortured to death" he all but growls through clenched teeth. You begin to reel slightly as you hear those words... the same words that have been echoing in your brain. Of course you know that it is not a possibility. In this country we don't allow criminals to be tortured, much less tortured to death; but you take a small comfort in the fact that the judge feels the same way. Your heart is now pounding inside your brain in anticipation of the next sentence. The judge lowers his head for a moment, and then looks back at the criminal. This time however, the hatred is missing from his eyes and a quiet calm has washed over his features. "That's what you *deserve*" he begins, "but I have the hope that there is still some good left in you. If you ever appear in this court again on similar charges, all the books that can be thrown at you will be. It is my desire that you learn from this and that you grow into an upstanding, productive member of our society. For that reason, I am going to allow you to walk away from this court a free man. Case dismissed!"

Ice water flows through your veins. Your skin pales a ghostly white as you slump into your seat. You want to jump up and scream out in protest, but your legs fail you. The cacophony of gasps, screams and moans from the courtroom threaten your sanity as the room begins to spin. The sickening swirl slows for a moment, and you open your eyes to see the object of your hatred looming over you. "You Christians should be happy for me!" he smirks "My judge has shown me mercy just like your judge showed you!"

The question is: are *you* happy for him? Do you feel vindicated for your daughter? Or do you feel that this is the biggest miscarriage of justice that you could ever have imagined? The reason that you want to vomit right now is because justice has not been served to you and your family. Yes, the perpetrator was shown mercy; just the way that you hope to be shown mercy by God... but how could this mercy feel so evil? The reason that you're feeling sick is because you have been denied justice. Without justice, mercy can become an instrument of evil. Yet, without mercy, justice becomes a cruel taskmaster.

Now there can be an infinitesimal glimmer of understanding of the position that God rules from. Before the crucifixion, mercy could only be found at the mercy seat. There was not a wide-spread policy of mercy, because in so doing, justice would have been denied. God is merciful, but he is also just. Throughout the justification period of the Old Testament God was unable to provide a blanket covering of mercy. When there was no hope left, God Himself provided the solution to the conundrum. In order to show mercy to all, the price of justice had to be paid by all. When there was no one found who could pay such a price, the word of God became flesh and dwelt among us. Then He gave His life, both to fulfill the penalty of the law in order to provide justice; and to pave a pathway of forgiveness through repentance in order to show mercy.

I was inspired to write the analogy in this chapter after reading a book called <u>The Shack</u>. I didn't write it, nor do I have any vested interest in the sale of the book. I want you to read the book because it is the most powerful writing that I have ever read that explores who God is. Because of my theological background, I had problems with the concept of the book. It is not theology, and it can't be read as such… but it was never meant to be. It is a fictional novel that paints the relationship that God longs for. Do as I did. I chose to set my theology aside, and just accepted and read the book for what it is.

I was brought to tears more times than I can count. The Shack concentrates the love in the heart of God found throughout the Bible, and pours it out more so than any one book of the Bible, or any author that I have ever read. Before you can continue down the pathway toward the Kingdom, you have to have a good understanding of who God is, how badly He wants to have a relationship with us, and how far He'll go to establish it. The Shack has the potential to change your life. It will take you from the understanding that God is the ruler of the universe, to a place where you can call him your father and understand what it is to bask in the pure, unadulterated, heartfelt love of a daddy.

You might have already been warned to stay away from it by your religious friends; but how badly do you want to know the heart of God? While it may not be what the religious world considers theologically correct, it is Biblical in how it presents Father's heart. Besides, who on earth can tell us exactly the manner in which God might choose to reveal Himself to us? He's already chosen a burning bush, a dove, a newborn infant, a pillar of cloud... nothing should shock us!

His Beauty Revealed

Transitions will come! Life is not static. God points toward tomorrow, and sometimes all we see is an impossible situation. In that impossibility lies an opportunity for God to show us His power!

There comes a moment to commit to moving forward, to step out, to risk it all. In those moments we discover who God is and the depth of His love for us. Sometimes even more exciting is the opportunity to find out who we really are!
- Richard Oliver

The prophet Isaiah gives us God's word:

When you're in over your head, I'll be there with you. When you're in rough waters, you will not go down. When you're between a rock and a hard place, it won't be a dead end— Because I paid a huge price for you. Isaiah 43:2-3 (The Message)

This photo came about as I was taking my family out to Ohio's Lake Vesuvius to see one of the Lord's hidden treasures that my husband and I had found. This trip was much to the delight of our daughter, but to the chagrin of our technologically advanced teenage sons. Free time to them was better spent online, and in no way shape or form had anything to do with being outside. To their amazement, they had a wonderful time. There was a moment when I couldn't find my youngest son, so I called out "Where are you?" "Exploring!" he replied from behind a giant rock. I would never have thought that my sons, who spend most of their free time in front of a computer or video game system, would take to exploring in the woods. They were taking risks, stepping out of their comfort zones and actually enjoying the great outdoors!

After an amazing afternoon, we all loaded up into our van and headed back home along the curvy roads of Southern Ohio. I was reflecting our beautiful day, when suddenly the Lord parted the clouds to give us one last beautiful kiss and shone His glory down in our path. Thank God for the curves and bumps in the roads. You never know where God will reveal His beauty to us.

—Lissa / Rock Hill, OH

This image may be freely downloaded for personal use at www.kingdomcultureministries.org

Chapter 8
Who Am I?

Who am I that you are mindful of me… that you hear me when I call? Is it true that you are thinking of me? How you love me. It's amazing, so amazing, it's amazing… I am a friend of God.[1]

So, did you read The Shack? You are truly doing yourself a disservice if you didn't. Knowing who God is and how badly He wants a relationship with us is paramount to understanding the Kingdom teachings of Jesus. If you don't start with that cornerstone of knowledge, then whatever you build is going to fall. After reading The Shack, you'll understand the heart of God like nothing else will ever be able to explain it to you. I can't stress enough how important it is to know God's heart.

After you know how much God wants a personal one-on-one relationship with you, the next step is: knowing who you are. You might think it a ridiculous concept, but the sad fact is: we don't know who we are. Just think about this for a moment. Let's say that a stranger calls you on the telephone. Perhaps it's for a new job interview, someone that you're just being introduced to, a relative that you've never spoken with, any number of reasons that a stranger might call; and she makes this statement: "so… tell me who you are". What would you say? Here's a task to complete before you go any further. Think about what your reply would be to "who are you?" You might even want to get a pen and paper and jot down a few things. Go ahead… I'll wait, and I promise to meet you in the next paragraph when you return.

Did you find this a little harder task than what you had first anticipated? The first thing that usually comes to mind for a working person is their job or career. When asked the question, they might say "I'm a union electrician", "I'm a beautician", "I'm a registered nurse" and of course there's no end to the jobs that could be listed. Is that the first thing that you thought of to explain who you are? The only problem with this answer is that it's not who you are... that is what you do.

Perhaps you're a student, a stay at home mom, a retired person, an unemployed person, a church volunteer, a youth minister, a Boy Scout or Girl Scout leader or... but again, these are things that you do. While you might be defined somewhat by the things that you do, the things that you do should never define you. Others might answer the question by stating their hobbies or interests. "I'm an amateur musician, I'm a stamp collector, I'm on the company softball team, I am a volunteer at the homeless shelter", etc. Again, these are things that you do, not who you are. Now are you finding it a little bit more difficult to describe who you are to someone? Some might describe themselves by saying "I collect antique cars" or "I'm married with two children", or "I own a day care center". Again, things that you have or that you own are not who you are. So, who are you? Let's investigate what the Scripture says.

In Jeremiah chapter 1, the prophet hears these words directly from the Lord: *Before I formed you in the womb I knew you, before you were born I set you apart* - Jeremiah 1:5 (New International Version). In the 139th Psalm, David writes: *For you created my inmost being; you knit me together in my mother's womb. I praise you because I am fearfully and wonderfully made; your works are wonderful, I know that full well. My frame was not hidden from you when I was made in the secret place. When I was woven together in the depths of the Earth, your eyes saw my unformed body. All the days ordained for me were written in your book before one of them came to be* - Psalm 139:13-16 (New International Version).

This makes it clear that whoever and whatever you are, you are known by God. Not only are we known, but we were known before birth. Before we took our first breath, God could look down the path that our life was going to take and see the choices that we would make. He could speak of those choices that we would make as existing, even before we were born. In writing an epistle to the Romans, the apostle Paul worded it this way: *As it is written: "I have made you a father of many nations." He is our father in the sight of God, in whom he believed—the God who gives life to the dead and calls things that are not as though they were* - Romans 4:17 (New International Version)

As we were in the mind of God even before we were born, that means that God actually thought about us and watched our lives unfold before we ever came into existence in the flesh. Pastor Scott Whaley has coined the term "God-thought" to refer to this. He empowers Christians into their identity by referring to them as a God-thought. What bad thing could come from the mind of God? If you answered nothing, then we are all perfectly created, coming out of the mind of God. Of course, we choose to turn away from that perfection; but that doesn't change the fact that we started out life as pure perfection in the mind of God. Before we were flesh, we were a God thought.

It gives me chills to know my heritage, and to know that I can refer to the God of all creation as "Father". Before I existed, He had birthed me in his mind. Still, it amazes me how much we have been lied to by the enemy, and how much of it we believe. Our identity has been stolen through lies and deceit. That's why it's so difficult for us to answer the question "Who are you?" ...because we truly don't know. We truly don't know who we are. We are being held captive to lies.

You've picked up quite a story and you've changed since the womb. What happened to the real you, you've been captured but by whom? *Bob Dylan - Property of Jesus - Shot of Love Copyright © 1981 by Special Rider Music*

When God looks at us, He sees us in our perfection through the blood. He no longer sees sin. He sees our true identity. To regain our identity in our own eyes, we need to turn to the Scripture. For far too long we have been told things that simply aren't true. For far too long we have been kept under rules and regulations, and been bound up in the chains of statements like: "I'm just a sinner saved by grace". That statement is nowhere to be found in the Bible. To find a statement that even alludes to something close to that, you would either have to reinterpret the Scripture or take it out of context. As an example, one place that has been taken out of context is in Paul's epistle to the Romans: *So I find this law at work: When I want to do good, evil is right there with me. For in my inner being I delight in God's law; but I see another law at work in the members of my body, waging war against the law of my mind and making me a prisoner of the law of sin at work within my members. What a wretched man I am!* - Romans 7:21-24 (New International Version).

The religious world continually takes this passage, as well as others out of context, and claims that the apostle Paul lived in sin everyday; or at least struggled with it every day. In actuality, Paul is juxtaposing the Christian life to a life under the law in order to show the Romans how much bondage they are in under the law, and how much freedom exist as a disciple of Christ. Remember, Paul was a devout Pharisee who tried to live a proper, Godly life under the law. As he is talking to the Romans, when he makes statements such as "When I want to do good, evil is right there with me", he is speaking about how difficult it is to live a life under the law. Because it's written in first person, many assume that Paul is communicating that he currently... at the moment he is writing... is feeling trapped in a world where he is a prisoner of the law of sin. That's quite a contradiction from him telling the Corinthians in book 2 chapter 5 that he was a new creation, or that: *"God made him [Jesus] who had no sin to be sin for us, so that in him [Jesus] we might become the righteousness of God"*- II Corinthians 5:21 (New International Version).

This concept is an easy thing to see when you look at the writings of Paul as a whole, rather than just misrepresenting one or two verses. For instance, he also wrote to the Romans: *Sin shall not have dominion over you; for ye are not under the law, but under grace.* - Rom. 6:14 (King James Version). However, you don't have to look very far to realize that Paul is not speaking about being trapped in sin in his current day-to-day life. All you have to do is to continue reading in Romans. The Scripture that was quoted earlier ended with verse 24. However, if you will continue to read even as far as the next verse, you can quickly understand his meaning, and see that he is talking about a lifestyle that he has been removed from.

What a wretched man I am! Who will rescue me from this body of death? Thanks be to God—through Jesus Christ our Lord! Romans - 7:24-25 (New International Version).

So, it sounds all doom and gloom and as if Paul is struggling with sin every day if you don't read the entire passage in context while realizing that he is writing in the first person about events of the past. Another thing that proves this concept is to start reading at the very beginning of chapter 7. Paul tries another way to teach the Romans that they are no longer living in sin every day if they have died in Christ. Here's a task for you to complete: get your favorite translation of the Bible and read Romans chapter 7 through its entirety. Before you read the Scripture, as always, pray for guidance and understanding from the Holy Spirit. Once you have finished, obtain copies of other translations of chapter 7 and re-read it. One easy way to compare various translations of verses or chapters is to go to the website www.biblegateway.com. There you'll find it easy to compare, not only different English translations, but translations in other languages as well. If you are only comparing one verse at a time, a more scholarly website to visit would be www.biblos.com. You will find some incredibly powerful references, commentary and translations there, as well as other scholarly tools.

Why would it be in anyone's best interest to read only to verse 24 of Romans chapter 7, and leave out the next verse in which Paul states that he has been rescued from that body of death? The reason is simple, but also very complex. Protestant churches have all been established and built upon rules and regulations to control their members. Of course, we are supposed to be in control, we are supposed to be under self-control. If we were all to live a life of self control, there would be no need for the law... or for any type of law, for that matter.

However, if you take the control away from the pastors, or the church board, or whoever sits at the head of the church; then they no longer have the ability to decide how you should live, or when and where and to whom you should give your money. Suddenly your freedom of self-control becomes an imposing threat to the system, so it simply cannot be allowed. The other factions that have no interest in seeing the Scripture quoted properly and completely, are those who are caught up in an endless religious nightmare of sin and punishment. They have never fully understood that once grafted into the dispensation of grace, the law became fulfilled. The work of Christ was not to do away with the Law of Moses, but it was to complete the law.

Christ didn't fail in his mission. He fulfilled the requirements of law. In his words: *"Think not that I am come to destroy the law, or the prophets: I am not come to destroy, but to fulfill "* -Matthew 5:17 (King James Version). So, with the law being fulfilled, there is no more law to condemn you. If there is no law, how would you be able to break the law? If you are unable to break any type of law, how can you sin? Let's read a passage from the book of John.

Then the scribes and Pharisees brought to Him a woman caught in adultery. And when they had set her in the midst, they said to Him, "Teacher, this woman was caught in adultery, in the very act. Now Moses, in the law, commanded us that such should be stoned. But what do you say?" This they said, testing Him, that they might have something of which to accuse Him. But Jesus stooped down and wrote on the ground with His finger, as though He did not hear. So when they continued asking Him, He raised Himself up and said to them, "He who is without sin among you, let him throw a stone at her first." And again He stooped down and wrote on the ground. Then those who heard it, being convicted by their conscience, went out one by one, beginning with the oldest even to the last. And Jesus was left alone, and the woman standing in the midst. When Jesus had raised Himself up and saw no one but the woman, He said to her, "Woman, where are those accusers of yours? Has no one condemned you?" She said, "No one, Lord." And Jesus said to her, "Neither do I condemn you; go and sin no more" - John 8:3-11 (New King James Version).

The religious world has always read the final verse to mean "You had best straighten up and start living right. You had better quit doing bad things". There are even a couple of English translations of the Bible that translate it in such a manner as to bias the reader towards that outcome. The Message, for example, translates it as *"From now on, don't sin"*. Is this what Jesus actually said, or was he saying: "You have called me your Lord, and therefore I will forgive your sins". This is something for you to pray about, for if I gave you my answer, I would be telling you *what to think* instead of *how to think*. Some things to consider while you're praying and pondering: there are one or two English translations of the Bible that don't translate 'Lord' as such. The transliteration of the Greek word used here is *kurie*. This word is virtually always translated as 'Lord'. It's a vocative case word, which has no equal in the English language. Basically, a vocative word is one in which the pronoun or descriptive word used identifies the particular person that it is in reference to. For instance, there are many lords just as there are many ladies. Being in the vocative case, however, indicates that the adulteress was referring to Jesus as *her* Lord and Master.

Whether you believe the phrase "sin no more" to be Jesus instructing the woman to live a perfect life or to translate that Jesus had the ability to wipe away all of her past and future sin to the point where there was no more sin; the bottom line is that He was stating that she should go forward in her life without sin. We will discuss this in detail later on.

For me to sum up this chapter is for me to answer the question "Who am I?"

1. I am a being that originated in the mind of God (Psalm 139:16).

I have accepted Christ as my personal savior and I call Jesus my Lord and Master, therefore:

2. I am dead to the law, and do not have to answer to it (Romans 7:3) (Romans 6:14).

3. I am a new creation (for the old one has passed away) (II Corinthians 5:17).

4. I am the righteousness of God (II Corinthians 5:21).

Suddenly, I'm beginning to feel a little better about myself!

Chapter 9
What Am I Doing Here?

Are you still feeling good about yourself? Religion has always attempted to make us feel bad about ourselves. It leaves a bad taste in the mouth, full of all the rules and regulations; all the things that you can't do anymore; all the right things that you have to start doing now; all the ways that you have to dress, and the ways that you are no longer able to dress. "You have to cut your hair / you're not allowed to cut your hair". "You can't wear jeans / you have to wear a dress". You can't say bad words, you can't drink a beer, you can't even *think* about the opposite sex... much less masturbate! As a matter of fact, you can't even say the word masturbate again. You have to be in church every Sunday morning, every Sunday night, and every Wednesday night if you're going to keep God happy. Remember... He's watching every move you make, just waiting for you to mess up. You're not allowed to have money because it's evil to have money. Since you have no money, you're not allowed to have worldly possessions. You can't laugh, party, joke around or have a good time. Do you think Jesus had a good time on the cross? You are supposed to pick up your cross and follow him! Sure it's a miserable life down here... the disciples were tortured and killed! But once you die, you'll be able to wear a crown. Oh yes, and most importantly you have to go tell everybody else that they are sinners as well, and that they need to start going to church and start living right (as you are doing).

Dear God! Just kill me now! Is it punishment for being a sinner that I have to suffer through this life? Now, I'm supposed to get others to follow me into this way of living? Who in their right mind would want to give up a world full of fun, laughter, partying and good times to live the miserable existence described above? The answer is nobody! People don't want to live that way! If they did, they would be beating down the doors of the church to get in. Since they aren't… they have to be tricked. Some might get them to come to church by telling them about a play that the kids are in, and asking them to come to support the kids. (That's just one of the ploys… there's a lot more). After the play, the preacher might start to browbeat you to make you feel horrible about the ghastly torture that Jesus went through for you. How can you continue to sit there in comfort when you know that He was beaten beyond recognition? Do you want to burn in hell? Do you want to suffer every second of every minute of every day throughout all of eternity? "With every head bowed, and with every eye closed… with nobody looking around… if you know there is some sin in your life… just slip your hand up real quick and you can put it right back down. Nobody here is going to embarrass you. I see that hand."

Even though you were told that no one is going to embarrass you, when people start looking around again, the preacher will say "Now, if you slipped your hand up, I want you to come up here to the altar and let us pray with you." He already saw you slip your hand up, now he's looking right at you… so you have to go. "Holy crap… what am I doing?" You think as you start to stand. "I only came here because this cute girl invited me… and I was hoping to get lucky tonight!" The pattern repeats itself over and over again, all across America, and across the world. It's sad to think of the tens of thousands of people who have only this recollection of what church is. There are hundreds of thousands of others who see Christians as preaching one thing, and then living the exact opposite. "Hypocrites! Why would I ever want to go to a church like that?" they say to themselves. "Those people at that church are mean and nasty and always have their noses in the air."

Well, this is the part of the book where we start to shake things up a little bit. We've always been told what to think as far as becoming a Christian and living a Christian life goes. Below are only a handful of the things that you might have heard or been taught.

I have always heard that:

1. The pinnacle goal of a life lived for the Lord is to go to the altar, pray for salvation, get baptized and start living a right life for Him.

2. For the somewhat fanatical, if we are bold enough, we could witness to someone by inviting them to our church. While in church... they might get saved as well.

3. We are only sinners that have been saved by grace.

4. A Christian needs to live right in order to be a witness to others. She should never go to bad places, do bad things, or hang out with bad people.

5. He should never say curse words, never drink alcohol, never smoke cigarettes or do other bad things to hurt his testimony.

6. She should always be in church Sunday morning, Sunday evening and Wednesday evening. God doesn't want to see empty church pews, because Christians need to fill the church pews in order to get fed the word of God.

7. New Christians need to be told to quit doing the things that they did in the world, and be reminded to live holy... as He is holy.

8. If an older Christian sees a young Christian doing something that he shouldn't, the new convert should be reprimanded and shown the right way to do things.

9. Read the Bible as often as possible, as that is the way in which God speaks to us today.

10. Jesus gave us a commission to go into all the world and get them saved. We should tell them that hell was made for the devil and his followers, but they are going to end up there if they don't turn their lives around.

11. Since we are only sinners saved by grace, we are going to keep sinning every day. But we need to try to stop it. God commands us to be holy and righteous. We need to fight

against our flesh every day, and work to keep it in line with the Word of God.

12. The Christian walk is not easy. If it were easy everyone would do it. The path is straight and narrow and the walk is hard; but if we keep struggling, if we fight the good fight and continue marching towards the goal... we will one day get our reward in Heaven.

13. If you're no longer getting fed the meat of the word found in this list, your pastor might have wimped out, or sold out to the WCC. Leave that place and go find a God-fearing church where you will get fed.

14. If you are not in church getting fed... you are going to starve to death spiritually. Seven days without church makes one weak.

How many of these have you heard before? There are so many hundreds of others that I could be writing down, but to tell you the truth, I have to stop before I throw up. These things are not what Christ has in store for you! These are lies of the enemy designed to break your spirit and keep you powerless, and to keep you glued to a church pew where you will wither away. Have you ever been wrong about anything? What if... and just humor me for a minute... what if there have been things that you've been taught in church and about church that just don't line up with Scripture? As you were reading through the sayings in this chapter, you might have been saying to yourself "that's true... I've seen that happen." Or "Yep, been there, done that!" Or maybe even "You know... when you actually see it written down in black and white, it doesn't sound so good as it does in church. Surely there is something more. Surely there is something better than this."

Here's another task for you, and it's a very important one before you continue reading. Pray this prayer with me from your heart: "Father (or, Papa or Daddy... whatever you're comfortable with) I'm just so sick and tired of all this crap. I'm tired of being miserable. I'm tired of wanting to do the right thing and wanting to live for you and never being able to do it. I'm tired of being confused. I'm tired of everyone telling me that their way of church is the right way. I just want to know the truth. From the bottom of my heart I cry out to you. Lord, as I continue to read this chapter, if it's not of you, I want nothing to do with it. I'm your child, and I am putting all my trust in you… and I know that you will not lead me down the wrong path. If these words don't speak your truth, then strike them from my mind. But, if what I read is a real… if what I read here is truth… if this is truly how I can live for you… then show me. Right now God, I'm putting all of my trust in you. Holy Spirit, as I continue to read, if this is of you… let my spirit bear witness. Let the spirit in me leap for joy and cry out yes, yes, yes! Then I will know. Then I will believe, because I'm asking these things in the name of Jesus. Amen!

If you've read The Shack, then you know how much God is in love with you and how badly He wants to communicate with you, and how much He just wants to be your friend. Of course I know that it's just a fictional novel, and of course I know that God probably doesn't take those forms… but who's to say? It's neither here nor there as far as what the basic message of the book is about. The book is about trying to convey the heart of God to us; just the way that it's borne out in the Scripture. It does an incredible job! Have you ever heard God described in such a loving manner… and with such care and concern for the human condition? You most likely won't. That's why it's such an incredible witnessing tool… because it gets you to the heart of your Creator. That's what He wants for you… but who are you? What are you doing here? Could it be that you're something more than what you've ever been told?

In the previous chapter we saw from the Scripture that you originated in the mind of God (Psalm 139:16). We read about how you are dead to the law, and do not have to answer to it (Romans 7:3) (Romans 6:14). And finally, we learned that you are a totally new creation (II Corinthians 5:17), and that God sees you as His righteousness (II Corinthians 5:21). The list of rules and regulations, and the ways in which a church member is supposed to act or not act that you read about earlier in this chapter need to be thrown in the trash. I challenge you to find any of that stuff in the Word of God. Let me just tell you in advance, in order to save you some time… none of that is in the Bible. That's the way man has created church. God doesn't want you in church… He wants you in a relationship… with Him. Once you get the relationship right, it is a good thing to gather together with other Christians. The Word tells us to do this (Hebrews 10:25).

Let's talk about some of the other things that are and are not in the Scripture.

It's simply not scriptural that we are sinners saved by grace. The Bible says: *But God showed his great love for us by sending Christ to die for us while we were still sinners* - Romans 5:8 (New Living Translation ©2007). Back when we were still sinners? So, this means that we are no longer sinners? We are not. We are the righteousness of God! So how is it that we can no longer sin? It's not that we have been made perfect while we are still on this Earth, and are now blameless without any sins. It's that we have died in Christ. Now... if we are dead, we are no longer under the law because the law has no effect and no consequences for a dead person. Let me give you an example. A woman who is lawfully married is bound to her husband as long as he is alive, but if her husband dies, she is released from the law of marriage. So then, if she marries another man while her husband is still alive, she is a bigamist and called an adulteress. But if her husband dies, she is released from that law and is not an adulteress, even though she marries another man.

So, my brothers and sisters, you also died to the law through the body of Christ that you might belong to another, to Him who was raised from the dead, in order that we might bear fruit to God. For when we were controlled by the sinful nature, the sinful passions aroused by the law were at work in our bodies, so that we bore fruit for death. But now, by dying to what once bound us, we have been released from the law so that we serve in the new way of the Spirit, and not in the old way of the written code.

In Corinthians, Paul writes: *"Everything is permissible for me"—but not everything is beneficial. "Everything is permissible for me"—but I will not be mastered by anything* - I Corinthians 6:12 (New International Version).

We have been set free from sin. The problem is that the church world doesn't understand the concept. Because of this, we are always in turmoil. We believe that we constantly have to run to the altar to beg forgiveness for our sins. We hear hellfire and brimstone preachers telling us that we'll go to hell if we keep it up. Dead people don't sin, my friend! Once we realize this, there is a peace and freedom and love of God that floods over us like nothing else imaginable. We are free from sin because we are already covered by grace. Of course, with that freedom we must exercise self control. We can't abuse the freedom. We can't say to ourselves "let's purposely sin! It's okay because we're covered by grace!" In writing to the Romans, Paul states it like this: *What shall we say then? Are we to continue in sin so that grace may increase? Of course not! How can we who died as far as sin is concerned go on living in it?* - Romans 6:2 (New International Version).

Let's consider this from another angle. Think of one of the people you love most in your life. It could be your husband or wife, your child, your mom or dad or your grandparent... it doesn't matter who it is, just think of that person that you love. Now imagine this: you say that you love this person with all your heart, but you're always watching them to try to catch them messing up. When they do something that you don't like, you punish them. You give them the cold shoulder and make them beg you to get back in your good graces. Do you do those things? Do you treat your children or your parents this way? Because if you do, then you don't understand what love is. *Love is patient, love is kind. It does not envy, it does not boast, it is not proud. It is not rude, it is not self-seeking, it is not easily angered, it keeps no record of wrongs. Love does not delight in evil but rejoices with the truth. It always protects, always trusts, always hopes, always perseveres. Love never fails* - I Corinthians 13:4-8 (New International Version). So, if you love your parents, or if you love your children; then you aren't looking for them to mess up so that you can turn your love away from them! *Love does not delight in evil but rejoices with the truth. It always protects, always trusts, always hopes, always perseveres. Love never fails.*

You are only human, yet you understand the concept of love well enough to know that your love ones are going to make mistakes. But you're not cruel to them when they do. You don't make them get on their knees and beg for your forgiveness every time they slip up... why? Because you love them. Man has an evil sin nature, but God does not. Think about this: *"Which of you, if his son asks for bread, will give him a stone? Or if he asks for a fish, will give him a snake? If you, then, though you are evil, know how to give good gifts to your children, how much more will your Father in Heaven give good gifts to those who ask him!* - Matthew 7:9-11 (New International Version).

Even with our carnal, sinful nature; we don't treat *our* loved ones the way that we've always thought that God treated *us!* How would you like it if you had a relationship with your young daughter, in which she saw you as a cruel taskmaster? What if she believed that she had to constantly run to you and say things like "Mommy, please forgive me! I didn't mean to fart in my brother's face! Please forgive me mommy! Please don't stop loving me! Please, mommy, please forgive me! Please don't hate me because I fart!"

Of course, the first time you might have to smile and think it's cute. But when you start to see the fear in her eyes as she begs you time after time not to hate her... it begins to tear at your heart. You just want to hold her in your arms and tell her that you love her, and that you will always love her, and that she doesn't have to keep begging you for forgiveness... simply for being human. You know that she's human, and you love her in spite of the fact. You just wish that she would quit begging you for love and understanding, and just realize that it's already there. It was already given to her... long before she even knew how to ask for it. You don't want her to beg. You just want her to crawl up in your lap and throw her arms around your neck and love on you; and thank you for being her mommy, and thank you for all the wonderful things that you do for her. If you are a mommy or a daddy... which relationship do you want with your child? Let's paraphrase and sum up the above verses from Matthew: *If you, then, though you are evil, know how to love your children, how much more will your Father in Heaven give love to those who ask him*! - Matthew 7:11 (New International Version. Paraphrased by Pinky).

So, what are you doing here? Why are you here at the altar begging God to forgive you and to please keep loving you? As far as God is concerned, there's nothing more to forgive. It's already been forgiven. He doesn't want you to keep beating yourself up, He wants you to crawl up in his lap and throw your arms around His neck and call Him Daddy and tell Him how much you love Him. That's the secret to living the life that He has created for you. The secret is that He's not out to punish you. He doesn't even know what you're talking about when you keep begging for His forgiveness. He just wants a relationship with you. That's it, pure and simple. He doesn't care if you ran a red light. It doesn't bother him that you looked at a dirty picture, or said a curse word, or drank some beers after work, or didn't go to church for two weeks, or lied to your uncle, or haven't read the Bible in over a year, or even that you farted in your brother's face. He created us, and knows that we are human. We cannot surprise or shock Him by what we do. He only wants that relationship.

So what about Sin? The only two things that you need to remember about sin are these:

1. If you keep begging forgiveness for it, then you are always keeping it in your mind. The longer that you keep it in mind; the more you're going to think about it. The more that you

think about it, the more likely it is that you will think about *doing* it again. Once you *think* of doing it, you will *want* to do it. If you *want* to do it, you're going to eventually do it. It's simply human nature. If something is placed directly in front of us, we are going to want it. So, keep it out of your mind. Stop holding onto it all week just so you can run to the altar with it on Sunday. Put it out of your mind. Out of sight, out of mind. Out of mind, out of heart.

The second thing that you need to know is this:

2.   God doesn't want you to have to beg for His forgiveness or His love. He only wants you to accept it. He wants you to enter into a love relationship with Him. Once you're in a relationship, and everything is going great, and you are so in love... you just start to want more and more of it. The more love you start feeling, the more you want. The more you want, the more you get. The more you get, the less that sin starts to be appealing in your life. Once sin becomes unappealing, you won't want to do it as badly as you once did. The less desire you have to do something... the less it will happen.

This is how we stop sinning. We cannot do it by focusing on the sin and continually begging forgiveness for it. We can't keep it in front of us all the time and expect not to want it. Instead we have to focus on our relationship with our Father. We need to pursue that relationship with all of our heart. Being a Christian has nothing to do with not being allowed to do this, or not being able to do that, or not being allowed to go to that place, or not being allowed to hang out with those people... it has nothing to do with sin or of trying to get rid of sin. It has everything to do with the pursuit of a love relationship.

From Barren to Bountiful

You are the bridge between history and His story. – Kris Vallotton

"And it came to pass, when they were gone over, that Elijah said unto Elisha, Ask what I shall do for thee, before I be taken away from thee."

"And Elisha said, I pray thee, let a double portion of thy spirit be upon me." "And he said, Thou hast asked a hard thing: nevertheless, if thou see me when I am taken from thee, it shall be so unto thee; but if not, it shall not be so."

"And it came to pass, as they still went on, and talked, that, behold, there appeared a chariot of fire, and horses of fire, and parted them both asunder; and Elijah went up by a whirlwind into heaven."

"And Elisha saw it, and he cried, My father, my father, the chariot of Israel, and the horsemen thereof. And he saw him no more: and he took hold of his own clothes, and rent them in two pieces."

"He took up also the mantle of Elijah that fell from him, and went back, and stood by the bank of Jordan; and he took the mantle of Elijah that fell from him, and smote the waters, and said, Where is The Lord God of Elijah? and when he also had smitten the waters, they parted hither and thither: and Elisha went over."

2 Kings 2:8-15(King James Version)

This old covered bridge was a hidden treasure that my husband and I happened upon on our way back from an amazing conference at the Covenant Church of Pittsburgh. The map and the GPS wanted us to drive an alternate route, but I allowed the Holy Spirit to be our guide on the way home. For once, we didn't have a deadline or a certain time to return home. We took the scenic route, and we were so glad that we did. This bridge just reminds me that we need to pick up the mantles of the great ones that have gone before us to provide a way for us to cross the waters. Their ceilings are our floors. We are to build upon what they have laid out for us. We need to be active participants in His story! What an amazing legacy!

—Lissa / The Knowlton Covered Bridge - Ohio Scenic Byway, Southern Ohio

Photo retouched by C. Deward at Lissa Pink studios

This image may be freely downloaded for personal use at www.kingdomcultureministries.org

Chapter 10
The Son of God

What do you suppose this chapter is going to be about... the son of God?

You are correct.

And who is this son of God? I mean... what is his name?

Now, you are incorrect.

This chapter is about you. *But as many as received him, to them gave he power to become the sons of God, even to them that believe on his name -* John 1:12 (King James Version). Do you believe on his name? Have you received him? Do you allow His Spirit to lead you? Then you are the son or daughter of God and this chapter is about you. *Because those who are led by the Spirit of God are sons of God -* Romans 8:14 (New International Version). This chapter is about your identity. Our identity has been stolen away from us, and we no longer realize who we are. Satan is a liar and a deceiver. Starting with the earliest recordings of his interaction with mankind, we read in the third chapter of Genesis how he used the crafty serpent to accomplish his goals:

Now the serpent was more crafty than any of the wild animals the LORD God had made. He said to the woman, "Did God really say, 'You must not eat from any tree in the garden'?"

The woman said to the serpent, "We may eat fruit from the trees in the garden, but God did say, 'You must not eat fruit from the tree that is in the middle of the garden, and you must not touch it, or you will die.' "You will not surely die," the serpent said to the woman. "For God knows that when you eat of it your eyes will be opened, and you will be like God, knowing good and evil"
-Genesis 3:1-5 (New International Version)

Satan didn't just come out with an outrageous lie that Eve could have easily seen through. He started slipping some thoughts in here and there, and used reason that sounded completely logical. That is the way that he has always worked. He slips in a little here and a little there, and before we know it, we start to believe and do the exact opposite of what God wants for us, and don't even realize it. As a matter of fact, we will fight and argue with other believers and point to Scripture (that Satan has so thoughtfully provided to us) in order to prove that we are right, and that our way is the correct way. After all, it says so right there in His word.

Remember that the devil knows the Scripture inside out, upside and down. He knows it better than any of us will ever know it. He doesn't simply make up lies about what the Scripture says, because that would not work. He realizes that all we would have to do is simply look it up. His specialty is quoting Scripture word for word, but at the wrong time or in the wrong place. The most devastatingly deceptive lie is telling the complete truth at the wrong time. The truth, spoken at the wrong time or in the wrong context becomes a lie. This is how Satan works. One example of this is recorded in the book of Matthew when Satan tempted Jesus in the desert: *Then the devil took him to the holy city and had him stand on the highest point of the temple. "If you are the Son of God," he said, "throw yourself down. For it is written: 'He will command his angels concerning you, and they will lift you up in their hands, so that you will not strike your foot against a stone.'"* - Matthew 4:5-6 (New International Version).

Satan is quoting Psalm 91:11-12 verbatim. Not only did he know the Scripture, but he knew it was written in reference to Jesus. This is why we have to be on guard against his treachery, and to continually pray and to allow ourselves to be led by the Spirit. Satan spoke the truth, and in the correct context; but Jesus was full of the Spirit, and realized that it was spoken at the wrong time. The truth spoken at the wrong time becomes a lie.

Let me give you a practical example of how Satan uses the word of God against us. You have surely read or been taught this Scripture: *For all have sinned, and come short of the glory of God* - Romans 3:23 (King James Version). When spoken of a nonbeliever, nothing could be truer. However, Satan takes this verse and puts it in front of Christians. It is a true verse, as are all Scripture; but spoken at the wrong time or to the wrong person, it becomes a lie. When Christians apply this verse to their own life, they are left feeling far less significant than the way God views them. In the previous chapter, we read that God doesn't see our sin when He looks at us; He sees the blood of Jesus. Therefore, to erroneously tell a Christian that he has sinned and fallen short of God's glory is a lie that does nothing but demoralize him.

There are so many examples that I could list. Virtually every Scripture could be made into a lie by using it inappropriately, at the wrong time, or directed toward the wrong person. Romans Chapter 7 is another Scripture that Satan has convinced Christians into thinking was written to them... with horrifically devastating results. Remember, Paul was talking about how difficult his life was before he met Christ. He always tried to be religious and do the right thing; but he found it impossible. He was not talking of living as a Christian, but of trying to be religious before he met Christ when he wrote: *For sin, seizing the opportunity afforded by the commandment, deceived me, and through the commandment put me to death* - Romans 7:11 (New International Version). *We know that the law is spiritual; but I am unspiritual, sold as a slave to sin. I do not understand what I do. For what I want to do I do not do, but what I hate I do* - Romans 7:14-15 (New International Version).

As it is, it is no longer I myself who do it, but it is sin living in me. I know that nothing good lives in me... for I have the desire to do what is good, but I cannot carry it out. For what I do is not the good I want to do; no, the evil I do not want to do—this I keep on doing - Romans 7:17-19 (New International Version). *So I find this law at work: When I want to do good, evil is right there with me. For in my inner being I delight in God's law; but I see another law at work in the members of my body, waging war against the law of my mind and making me a prisoner of the law of sin at work within my members* - Romans 7:21-23 (New International Version). *So then, I myself in my mind am a slave... to the law of sin.* Romans 7:25 edited (New International Version).

When you go through your entire Christian life being told that you are nothing more than a prisoner of sin... that even though you want to do good, sin will overpower you... and when you constantly hear "How do you think you could possibly escape your sinful nature when even the apostle Paul couldn't?"... You become beaten-down. If you grow up in an environment being told that you're worthless and will never amount to anything, it affects you in a negative way. You end up with a bad self-image, feelings of worthlessness and hopelessness, and a complete lack of confidence in yourself and in your abilities. The true you... your true identity... was stolen from you; but growing up in that environment is all that you've ever known, so it only seems natural. It seems right; but you don't even realize what has happened to you.

There is a horrifically devastating crime that has been perpetrated against Christians. Our identity has been stolen, and we have no clue that there was even a theft. In some minds, it is believed that there is no good in us and that we are worthless. We are poor, wayfaring strangers wandering through this land of woe. We know that we have to take up our cross and follow Him down the narrow pathway full of pitfalls and sorrows. When we stumble or become heavy laden, the best that we can pray in these times of turmoil is *"Oh God, if it be thy will... let this cup pass from me; but not my will O Lord, but thy will"*. We have been demoralized from every angle. We have been slapped, kicked, beaten, raped and burned by the enemy, and we just assume that it's part of being a Christian. We have to suffer just as Christ suffered, because we're nothing more than sinners saved by grace. I've even heard misguided Christians state that we are all little more than lowly worms in His magnificent creation.

It's sickening. It's truly gut wrenching to see the children of the Almighty wallow in such self loathing. It is mind numbing watching those who bear His name and stand to inherit His kingdom grovel in pity. Those who have been called as kings and high priests see themselves only as lepers and harlots. It's time to send up the battle cry! It's time to scream out "no more!" We have been lied to for far too long. It's the breaking of a new day. It's the dawn of a new season. Never again will we cower in fear at the lies we've been told. It's time that we stand and claim our inheritance. It's time to lay down the cross that we carry around. Of course Christ told us to take it up and follow Him, but follow Him to where? To His death! We follow Him to death in baptism, and then we raise from the death a new creature. We are to follow Christ, but He arose from death a new creature. He doesn't still lug the cross around.

As we read earlier in this chapter, the Scripture refers to us as God's children in John and Romans, but there are so many other scriptures that attempt to teach us our identity in Christ. I am only going to list a handful to give you an idea of how God views us.

We are more than conquerors: *Nay, in all these things we are more than conquerors through him that loved us* - Romans 8:37(King James Version).

We are victorious: *But thanks be to God, which giveth us the victory through our Lord Jesus Christ* - I Corinthians 15:57 (King James Version).

We are God's righteousness: *For he hath made him to be sin for us, who knew no sin; that we might be made the righteousness of God in him* - II Corinthians 5:21 (King James Version).

We are holy and blameless in His sight: *According as he hath chosen us in him before the foundation of the world, that we should be holy and without blame before him in love* - Ephesians 1:4 (King James Version).

We are seated with Christ: *And hath raised us up together, and made us sit together in Heavenly places in Christ Jesus* - Ephesians 2:6 (King James Version).

We are lights for the lost: *For ye were sometimes darkness, but now are ye light in the Lord: walk as children of light* - Ephesians 5:8-9 (King James Version).

He has made us Kings and Priests: *And hast made us unto our God kings and priests: and we shall reign on the Earth* - Revelation 5:10 (King James Version).

There are so many more that you will find as you read. God wants us to know our identity. He wants us to understand how powerful we are and how empowered we are to carry His good news to a lost and dying world. Not only does the Creator of the universe know us, He knew us from before the beginning of creation. Not only has He always known us, but He loves and adores us. Not only does He have immeasurable love for us, but He has made us powerful and given us the same identity as Jesus! We are His sons and daughters! We are children of the King! That makes us princes and princesses! We are made holy through Christ, and empowered to be his ambassadors on Earth. What an incredible calling! What fantastic gifts He has bestowed upon us! And most importantly, how incredibly opposite of what we've always been told! We are not weak! We are not powerless! We are not poor! We are not fatherless! We are not homeless! We have royal blood flowing through our veins, and the powers and riches of the Kingdom of Heaven at our fingertips!

Excellent Peace

Excellence is the result of caring more than others think is wise, risking more than others think is safe, dreaming more than others think is practical and expecting more than others think is possible.- Kris Vallotton quotes this, but the author is unknown.

And it shall come to pass afterward, that I will pour out my spirit upon all flesh; and your sons and your daughters shall prophesy, your old men shall dream dreams, your young men shall see visions:

And also upon the servants and upon the handmaids in those days will I pour out my spirit.

Joel 2:27-29 (King James Version)

I was at the 2010 prophetic conference in Redding, California hosted by Kris Vallotton, and was poured into by some of the most amazing people gifted in the prophetic. There were people from all over the world that attended that conference, and I made some of what I am sure will be lifelong friends like Mary, Renee, Kimmie and her sister Emily, Jason, Lewis, and Holli, the spitfire prophet of Mississippi. After fellowshipping with these amazing people, I went out to Whiskeytown Lake just outside of Eureka, California where I snapped this photo. In my mind, I was mulling over all the wonderful words of wisdom that I had heard. I was thinking of the mantles that had been passed on to us, and of the dreams about to be realized by us all. The most excellent peace came over me. I will never be the same, nor would I ever care to be. Now, I care more than others think wise, risk more than others think safe, dream more than others think practical and expect more than others think possible! Dream on, you dreamers as He pours His spirit out on us! How fortunate we are to live in this time, right here, right now!

—Lissa / Whiskeytown Lake, CA

This image may be freely downloaded for personal use at
www.kingdomcultureministries.org

Chapter 11
Call from God, Are We Reaching?

Hello? This is Heaven calling. Hello? I have a call for you from God, are we reaching? Hello?

God is trying to communicate with you. Are you listening? Do you know how to listen? Do you know what to listen for? To start with, it's a good thing for you to know and understand that God is in a good mood. He's having a never-ending good hair day. As we learned in Chapter 7, the big scary God of the Old Testament has softened. Yes, He is the same yesterday today and forever blah, blah, blah. The bottom line is: now there is mercy. Now He can show us His love completely. As you read in The Shack, He will go to any lengths to reach us... to communicate with us... to show us how much He loves us.

I recently told one elderly brother who was locked into his denominational thinking; that the Lord was aching to communicate with him. His reply was "The Lord talks to me through the Bible, and that's all I need." I felt so sorry for him, but I was unable to reach him. I received an owner's manual upon the purchase of my new Town and Country van. When updates started to come in the mail, I could have easily discarded them thinking that "I already have the manual, why should I need more". It turns out that those updates were vital for the safety of me and my family. Had I chosen to ignore them, it would not only have created a perilous situation for me, but for my loved ones as well. If you are the spiritual leader of your family, you can easily recognize the parallel. The Bible is what God was speaking 2000 years ago. What is He saying today?

Okay... time for another task. I want you to close this book for a few seconds, close your eyes, lie back and get comfortable if you are able; and think about the last wonderful vacation that you took. Take notice that I used the word "wonderful". If your last vacation sucked because you got into an argument with your in-laws... that's not the one I'm talking about! Think of the one before that. This is a serious task. Without reading the next paragraph, I want you to stop and think for a few seconds about your vacation. Picture where you were and all the sites you saw. Try to remember people, places and things that you witnessed. After a few seconds, come back and read the next paragraph. Don't worry. I'm not going anywhere.

Okay, now tell me... where did you go on your vacation? Really? No kidding? You are not going to believe this, but I can tell you all about it! Have I ever been there? No, I've never been there; but I've always wanted to go! I wasn't able to go, but I got a book about it at the library and I read all about it. So, you were amazed looking at the trees that had been laid over by the hurricane? Now wait, this picture that you took... that's not how they look! I know they don't look like that for a fact, because I looked at every picture in the book I read. You traveled on the interstate? Well, I'm sorry; but you must be mistaken. You can't travel that way because the road isn't finished. How do I know? I read it in my book! Didn't you listen?!

This one-sided conversation might sound a little goofy, but here's the point: I read about the place... you actually went there. If we were going to tell a mutual friend about the vacation, which one of us do you think would be more accurate? You see, you can read about things over and over and over again; but there's nothing that can compare to actually experiencing the thing that you're reading about. That's why I have adopted the motto: "Encounters are better than knowledge." You can't quote me on this one, because I'm not the first to say it... but it's a fantastic one to live by!

Have you been born again? Do you know that encounter? How many people are you going to listen to and believe, who tell you that there is no such thing? No matter how educated they are, no matter how much they've read, no matter how eloquently they can articulate an explanation of how the born-again experience is only a figment of the hyper imagination, brought on as the super-ego conquers the desires of the id.... are you going to, at some point, say "Well, now that you've explained it to me like that... I guess being born-again *can't* be real." Of course not! Why? Because you experienced it! Nobody can take that encounter away from you, regardless of how much talking they do.

This holds true with any experience that you can name. How aggravating is it when a single person who has never been married and never had children starts to lecture you on how to raise your child or take care of your spouse? Would you actually debate a brain surgeon on the feasibility of conscious sedation for glioma removal? Probably not, regardless of how much you've read about the subject.

When you are referencing an encounter, there is no one better to speak with than someone who has actually had the encounter. It just doesn't make any sense to listen to somebody who has never had the encounter, tell you that it can't be real simply because they haven't personally experienced such an encounter. And certainly, you don't want to debate them over it. Yet, time and time again Christians will argue and debate over whether encounters described in the Bible are still in operation today, when they themselves have never had the encounter. It's tantamount to someone arguing that the planet Mercury could not be real, because they've never seen it.

If you want to know the truth about a particular encounter, experience it yourself. Short of having your own encounter, speak with someone who has personally experienced it. It's absolutely pointless to listen to someone who has never had the encounter argue that the experience could not be real.

Well then, exactly how does God communicate with us today? Does he speak in an audible voice?

"I have never heard God speak in an audible voice".

So, then, if he doesn't speak in an audible voice, could He perhaps communicate...

"Hold on just a moment. I said '*I've* never heard God speak in an audible voice'."

"Yes... that's what I thought you said."

"Alright... okay, then I must've misunderstood you."

"So, since God doesn't speak to us audibly..."

"Wait now, what I said was that 'God doesn't speak to *me* audibly'"

"That's what I said"

"No, that's what *I* said!"

"Okay... that's where I heard it then. So, since God doesn't speak audibly, ***who*...**"

"Why do you insist on putting **Who** on third base?"

"**Who** am I putting on third base?"

"Yes, but we don't want him there!"

"You don't want ***who*** there?"

"No!"[2]

I'm sure that there are a few of you smiling right now, and the rest are totally confused. I apologize for slipping into some wonderful childhood memories, but the point that I'm making is that because I've not heard the audible voice of God doesn't mean He doesn't speak audibly. Obviously, there are instances recorded in the Bible in which He audibly spoke to mankind. It is recorded that He spoke audibly with at least Adam, Noah, Abraham and Moses... and speaking of Abraham, God asked him to sacrifice his son, Isaac. Abraham knew the word of the Lord and was prepared to carry it out. Thankfully, he was also in close enough relation to God to hear fresh words that the Lord had for him.

Of course, it would be easy enough to say that God spoke audibly with people in biblical times... but that He doesn't do that today. The only problem is that I have spoken with several people that have heard the audible voice of God. I have heard from people who are Spirit-filled, on-fire Christians who have nothing to gain, but perhaps a bit to lose by claiming to have heard the audible voice of God. I have no reason whatsoever to doubt their encounters or their testimonies.

How can any intelligent, thinking person debate on a subject while coming from a place of a lack of knowledge or understanding or experience about the subject? For me to state that God does not speak to man in an audible voice is tantamount to an atheist stating that God does not exist. By saying that God does not exist, one is stating by direct implication that "I have been everywhere in the universe, in every time period, and in no time period is there any creative being other than mankind". It's easy, then, to see the ludicrousness of a statement such as "There is no God".

If there is anyone who can honestly make the above claim… that they have been everywhere and seen every place in the universe that has ever existed in every past present and future realm of time, and have verified that there is no more powerful, more creative being than mankind in any of those places or time periods; then we would bow to them as God. In either case, the non-existence of God can not even be brought into intelligent debate. In the same vein of thinking, we cannot debate whether God speaks in an audible voice if we have never encountered it.

Therefore, until it can be proved otherwise, I will have to go on the encounters of those individuals who have always presented themselves sane and truthful in every other aspect of their lives, and conclude that at times God does use an audible voice to speak to some people. In the same breath however, I would not ask you to be on the constant listen for the audible voice of God. Even to those who have had the encounter, it is a rare occurrence, more times than not only happening once-in-a-lifetime.

Of course, God does indeed speak to us through His written Word. But remember, those words were not written by God Himself with His own hand… the Scriptures were written by men who were under the influence of the Holy Spirit. God was speaking to them through their spirit, and instructing them what to write. How does that work? If you are a born again believer who has been baptized in the Holy Spirit, then the Spirit of God lives within you. If you then pray earnestly to God - in the spirit - for understanding, knowledge or any other gift; He will freely give it. *And all things, whatsoever ye shall ask in prayer, believing, ye shall receive -* Matt.21:22 (King James Version). The writers of the New Testament were not writing a Bible, they were simply sending letters to various churches and individuals. Of course, they were writing under the influence of the Holy Spirit, as they had prayed for divine wisdom in order to be able to address the exact needs of those they were writing to.

Are we dealing with the same God today? Of course we are. Does He still freely give to those who believingly ask? Of course He does. I am born again. I am Spirit filled, and pray believingly in the spirit. Each time I sit down to write more of this book, I seek the face of the Lord in prayer. My prayer is usually something similar to this: "Father, please guide me and give me the words to write today. Use me, Holy Spirit. Guide my words so that I am speaking everything that you would speak, and nothing of myself. Let these words that I write be exactly what the reader needs at this moment in time, and let me write nothing of my own, but only those words from you."

The writers of the New Testament present us with proof that God speaks to man through the inspiration of the Holy Spirit. So if I pray in the Spirit, believing that God will inspire each word that I write, are you now reading the word of God? That's for you to decide. Am I comparing myself to the writers of the New Testament? Absolutely not. Am I claiming to be writing under the same authority and anointing as were they? Absolutely not. Am I claiming that the words in this book are just as much the word of God as the words in the Bible? Absolutely not. I'm not claiming anything. I am simply telling you my heart, and how I approach the heart of God, and how I pray in the Spirit for Him to use me in everything I say, do or write… for His glory.

Finally, and most importantly, there is a way in which God speaks to us constantly and continually that most people never think about and never even consider. It's what we have given the name 'coincidence'.

Mysteries Around the Bend

Every one of us was born to believe in what we can't see.

— Garner Tullis

Now faith is the substance of things hoped for, the evidence of things not seen.
Hebrews 11:1

Often times we see a path ahead of us, but we are uncertain of whether to move forward. It may be unfamiliar, and that is scary to some people. What if something bad were to happen? I used to think that way myself, but now I know the truth. I know that no matter what happens, *ALL* things work together for the good of those who believe. But, I now have faith that there *will* be something amazing around the bend, because Papa loves me, and He wants good things for me!

So, as I walked along this path, towards the "scary" cave, I began to see something so brilliant and beautiful inside. I felt as if I had been transported to another planet. I could not believe that the inside of a cave could be so utterly amazing and breathtaking! Even though I could not see it from the path, I believed He would show me something amazing around the bend. Thank you, Lord! Thank you for showing me this hidden treasure.

— Lissa/ Lake Vesuvius, Ohio

This image may be freely downloaded for personal use at
www.kingdomcultureministries.org

97

Chapter 12
What are the Odds?

God doesn't control us in any shape or fashion. He has given us complete free will to live as we desire. However, even if we do not accept the love he has for us... even if we continue to go against what we know in our hearts to be his desire for us... He still loves us. Just as parents love a child that has gone astray, and will always be there for them should they decide to change their ways, and will always try to communicate and be influential in their lives in whatever manner they are allowed to be... God is there for us. He tries to be influential in our lives. He tries to drop us hints that He is waiting for us and still loves us. These are supernatural events however. Man does not relate to the supernatural, as he has no logical explanation for it. While he sees something that can't be explained in logical terms happening all around him... attributing it to God would be venturing into the realm of the supernatural.

So, man gives these happenings the name 'coincidence'. They still can't be explained, they are still not logical, they are still outside the realm of human experience... but giving them a name and calling them random events that shouldn't have happened in logistical terms other than by chance, takes away the thinking that they could have been orchestrated by God. This takes away the supernatural element, and man is happy to go on his way. Sometimes though, we run into a situation like the one you read about in chapters one and two. I am an intelligent person with a healthy IQ. Were you to tell me that two random, unrelated events happened at the same time, whose resultant combination defies explanation; I could buy that. I could chalk that up to chance.

When you tell me that three or four or five or more random events, whose combination at a particular moment in space and time defies logical explanation; yet somehow all came together to produce an amazing result... I start to have a hard time with the randomness of it all.

When one starts to apply Kolmogorov's axiom of probability theory to linear mathematics, and numbers begin to exponentially increase; random chance soon loses its viability to even those with little or no mathematical background.

A 20th century scientist by the name of Richard von Mises introduced the concept of sample space into probability. Basically stated, sample space just takes into account the number of variables that could possibly exist within the particular subject or event being studied. For instance, if the subject was a deck of cards, and the variables were colors, the sample space would only reflect two, as there are only black and red. If the subject were suits, the space would be four. If it were picture cards it would be 12, etc. The space gets very confused however, when there are many different subjects each with many different variables. This is where exponential numbers come in and the odds are sometimes so astronomically huge that they become incalculable.

For instance, if I asked you to walk up to a random stranger of your own choosing... anywhere in the world that you so choose... what are the odds that their name would be Carmella? Substantially high odds against it wouldn't you think? Here's the deal I'll make for you. I will allow you to choose any random person. I will tell you ahead of time what their name will be... but it won't stop there. I will tell you ahead of time what their parent's names are (or were), the names of each of their grandparents, how many pets each of those seven people have had in their life, and the names of each of those pets. I'm not psychic, and I don't have any inside tricks for coming up with all of these names. I'm just going to leave it to random chance that I can come up with them. If I'm right with every single name; you owe me $300. If I'm wrong even on one of the names, I will give you $10,000.

Would you take my bet? Most likely it would matter little to you that you've never heard the name Andrey Nikolaevich Kolmogorov. You're not likely to be concerned if you don't know a whole lot about mathematical probabilities. What most likely will be running through your mind is "this guy is nuts! There is no way he can pick a random stranger and tell me all that information... it would simply be impossible!" So, assuming that it's not against your religious morals, you would most likely take me up on the bet, and you would be correct to do so. Even without knowing the complexities of the various theories of probabilities, you have quickly come to the conclusion of "That is impossible! It can't be done... I'll take your bet!"

There are so-called coincidences around us constantly. But what if they were actually something more than mere coincidence? Think about how the events came together in Tammy's story. There were so many things that could've gone so many different ways that it almost becomes impossible to believe that it wasn't orchestrated by an unseen hand.

I could literally tell you of thousands of these God-incidences in my life, because that is one way in which I communicate with and seek out the will of God. As there is neither time nor space to do so, I will leave you with just one... albeit an important one to me.

Before I tell it to you, this whole concept of God incidences may be something completely foreign to you, so let me tell you a little bit about how it works. Basically, it's simply asking God a question and looking for the answer that is provided in a series of events that you will understand. Sometimes I simply pray "God, give me a sign today as to what you want me to do." Sometimes I spend the day looking for a sign, and sometimes I forget about it until the sign appears. The sign could be anything, as long as it means something to you, and you can justify it and establish it in your own mind to be more than a random event.

If you start putting this method of communicating with God into practice, you might just find out that sometimes God has flair for the dramatic, and many times with a sense of humor as well! Consider this prayer: "Lord, you know my friend Sally is a lesbian. I love her, and I think that I am a great influence on her... but everyone at my church tells me that I need to stay away from her. I don't know what to do, Lord. I just want to be everything to you and for you and live how you would want me to live. If you don't want me to be around Sally, I don't want to be around her either. Dear Jesus, please show me a sign. I'll be looking for any type of sign, Lord, to let me know if I should stay away from my friend. I'm going to put this in your hands and trust you to give me an answer. I'll be looking for your answer in what people say or do or in whatever you want to give me to let me know your heart. Amen."

Megan asked for a sign from God. Sometimes God just wants to show off. Megan got in her car and drove 10 miles down a road that she had never traveled before. Suddenly she became giddy. She had to pull over to the side of the road. She laughed so hard that she began to cry... and cry... and then to weep uncontrollably. She sat there for 10 minutes crying so hard that she couldn't see to drive. She was finally able to calm down and wiped the tears away from her eyes enough that she could see it again. Directly in front of her was a huge billboard sign. It was nothing more than a completely black billboard with white letters that read: *Contrary to popular belief, I don't hate anyone who's gay - God.*

He-e-e-re's your sign. Yes, this is an actual billboard sign by the side of an actual road. You can go to Google images and type in something like: *God gay billboard* and then search the images. You should be able to see it in the first image or two.

Would you call that having a sense of humor? Would you call it having flair for the dramatic, or simply say that it was a coincidence? Another way to communicate with God in this manner is to give him a specific set of parameters to work within. Once when I needed an answer; but didn't particularly want the answer to be "yes", I came up with a request of God. My wife had been given a sign in California on this particular night of seeing a yellow Corvette. There might be a ton of yellow Corvettes in California, but I was traveling through rural Eastern Kentucky on this particular evening. A lot of pickup trucks; but no Corvettes... and definitely nothing yellow!

Inspired by Lissa's yellow Corvette sighting in California, and not really wanting to get an affirmative answer to my question, I said "Lord, if the answer to this question is to be "yes", show me a yellow pickup coming towards me in the other lane. I felt pretty safe on this one as I only had about 10 minutes to drive, and I could never recall ever seeing a yellow pickup truck in my life, much less seeing one in rural Kentucky. But, what a coincidence... five minutes later there was the prettiest sunflower yellow Ford pickup truck heading toward me that you could ever imagine. "Well if that isn't the darndest thing" said I. "Only in Morehead, Kentucky!"

Asking God to communicate with you in this manner is completely biblical. There are several instances throughout the scripture in which various people have asked God for a sign. In the sixth chapter of the book of Judges, all of the Midianites, Amalekites and other eastern peoples had joined forces in order to cross over the Jordan, camp in the Valley of Jezreel, and attack Gideon and the Israelites. Even though the Lord had promised him a victory, Gideon came up with a request of the Lord:

Gideon said to God, "If you will save Israel by my hand as you have promised- look, I will place a wool fleece on the threshing floor. If there is dew only on the fleece and all the ground is dry, then I will know that you will save Israel by my hand, as you said." And that is what happened. Gideon rose early the next day; he squeezed the fleece and wrung out the dew—a bowlful of water - Judges 6:36- 38 (New International Version).

Even after having assurance from the Lord however, and even after putting Him to the test through the fleece, Gideon persisted:

Then Gideon said to God, "Do not be angry with me. Let me make just one more request. Allow me one more test with the fleece. This time, make the fleece dry and the ground covered with dew." That night God did so. Only the fleece was dry; all the ground was covered with dew - Judges 6:39- 40 (New International Version).

We can see from the prayers of Gideon and many others in the Bible that God does give us signs when we ask for them. Gideon even went the extra step of asking two more times for two completely opposite signs, and got both of them. Of course... there are those that still might see the incidences of the fleece as mere coincidence. In the long run however, the answers were correct. God did indeed deliver victory to Gideon.

Now you have the key of communication. You know some ways that you can communicate with God that truly work. More keys remain, however before we get to them, I promised to tell you an all important communication that I had with the Lord. At the time I met my current wife Lissa, I was legally married to another. My wife had left me more than a year earlier, and was living three states away. Though she had not remained faithful to me, I had remained faithful to her because I thought it was the right thing to do. I was miserable. I love being married and I hate being on my own. I discovered something worse than wanting to be married while living alone, however... not wanting to live alone while being married.

Then I met Lissa. From the first words of our conversation, we hit it off instantly. We had so many things in common, and the differences that we had were things that seemed to complement a lack in the other one's life. It truly seemed to me, for the first time in my life, that there was actually someone who had been sent to the Earth just for me. However, I started to let rules and regulations get to me. I kept hearing in my mind "You are already married... what are you thinking?"

As much as I hated the thought, I felt that it would be the right thing to do to break off my friendship with Lissa, in hopes that my wife might return, and might stay more than the usual few months before she was off again. I prayed hard about it. I told God that I was going to do what I thought was the right thing by breaking off our friendship, and that if it was in His plans for Lissa and me to be together, He was going to have to give me a sign. I did not pray for anything specific, but I told the Lord that it was going to have to be a big one that completely blew me away, in order for me to understand. Otherwise, I would not see Lissa again.

While Lissa and I had been having a wonderful time together, and were incredible company for one another; we were still in the 'getting to know one another' stage. There was no talk of love, or of even staying together as a couple. She might have been told that I was married by the girl that introduced us... I'm not sure about that, but I did tell her within the first half hour of talking with her, so there was never anything hidden or brushed under the table between us.

As earnestly as I have ever prayed, I told the Lord one day that "Today is the day I am going to break it off with Lissa, before it goes too far into the realms of no turning back". I told Him that I would break it off unless He showed me a sign to the contrary. I had no idea what the sign was to be, but I was very specific with the Lord in telling Him that it had to be so huge as to completely catch me off guard and leave no doubt in my mind. I remember specifically saying things like: "Lord, I won't accept people kissing on a billboard, or passing a field of pretty flowers or a couple holding hands in the park"... In other words, "If you don't blow me away with a sign, I won't accept it as coming from you, and I will break up with Lissa."

The moment came... and no sign. We were riding in my Jeep, and I solemnly said "Lissa, there is something I need to talk to you about." "There is something I wanted to tell you, too" she replied in her charming little girl voice and mannerisms. "Well," I stuttered, "let me go first because mine's pretty important." "No, let me go first" she insisted, never being one to be able to sit on a secret. I relented, as I knew that she wouldn't. "Alright" No sooner had I mumbled out the word when she flipped open a small wooden case to reveal a diamond encrusted man's wedding band. As the glimmer caught my eye, she bubbled out "Will you marry me?"

That question can hit hard and shock someone into their senses even when they're expecting it. For me, it was as if I had just slipped into a surreal movie. "What did you do?" I halfway demanded. Keep in mind that I had never said "I love you" to her. I had never talked about marrying her... I was already married! "What did you do?" I stammered again, as I was forced to pull over to the side of the road. "I saw it in the store today" she said "and something told me that I had to buy it and ask you this today!"

"So... what's your answer?" The little girl inquired. I looked up towards Heaven, and then tried to focus on her through the tears. I finally choked out the simple "yes". We hugged, and giggled like school kids. When we finally got on our way, and still in the glow of the moment... she said "okay it's your turn, what did you want to say?" "Well, it must not have been that important after all!" I truthfully beamed, "because I can't remember it for the life of me!"

What a coincidence! God always answers prayer, and He's always right on time with the answer. These many years later, I can't imagine life without my best friend and ministry partner. The key of communication with God is an important one indeed. It's important to know what God did in the past, but it's imperative to know what He's doing right now.

The next key that you will need is the key of cultural understanding. You have to understand that there is a vast cultural difference in living in the Kingdom of God on Earth as it is in Heaven and in living in the traditional church culture as it has always been taught. It is almost as if they are diametrically opposed to one another. Coming into the understanding of the remarkably vast differences in church and Kingdom living can be difficult to those who have only known a church culture. Please understand that I am not coming out against the denominational churches. They are our legacy. There is no need to call for demise, only for enlightenment. That being said, I have to give the rule of thumb that if you have been attending one of the denominational churches, you have been brought up in church culture. You are the one that I'm speaking to about the hard transition. You don't have to leave your church, but you have to walk away from your culture in order to live the Kingdom life that Christ has prepared for you.

Believe me; I do understand the sacrifice that the Lord is requiring of you. I am a proud, born and raised American. I mean no offence what-so-ever, as I'm sure that you are just as proud of your homeland; but I see America as the greatest Country in the world in which to live. However, if the Lord called me out into another country, and told me to never return to the United States, I would do so without hesitation or regret. I would rather the Lord call me His own than be able to call myself an American, or a Japanese, or a Baptist, or a German, or a Pentecostal, or a nurse or any descriptive word that you can think to place here. If you don't truly belong to Him and walk in His Kingdom, then the name over your church door is of little value.

That paragraph was written many months ago. The manuscript for this book was already finished and turned over to the publisher, when an example of what I am writing about occurred in my own life. I had to request the editing to be put on hold in order to add these four paragraphs. Through a series of events that I will write about in a future book, God made it abundantly clear to my wife and me that we were to do the very thing that I had set forth in the above paragraph. The Lord doesn't push or demand, the Holy Spirit is a gentleman who simply asks. We were asked if we would walk away from our home, from the area of the Country where we live, from our church and ministry, friends and family, jobs and incomes in order to be at the Bethel School of Ministry for the 2011 year.

This was not in my plans in the least. Imagine sacrificing the very things that God had given you, the things that He had told you were to be your inheritance and legacy, in order to venture into the complete unknown because He was showing you something new. Abraham did that very thing, as have many men and women of God throughout history. I knew that it was not mandatory for me to follow the leading of the Holy Spirit. I could have stayed at home in my ministry, and God would have continued to bless it; but I wanted Him more than His gifts.

I am now writing these four paragraphs from Bethel. I have only been here for one week, and already author and teacher Kevin Dedmon prophesied that my ministry would change the world, and laid hands on me to receive his healing mantle that was handed down to him from Lonnie Frisbee. I was prophesied over by author and teacher Steve Backlund that I would be speaking to multitudes, and would open the eyes and hearts of the world using language and teachings that were easy for people to grasp (He knew nothing of this book at the time). He also gave me a copy of his book *Cracks in the Foundation*, which I highly recommend to every Christian.

I've also heard from Connie Deulley, head of Bethel Valpo Prophetic Ministry. She told me that God gave her a word that I was like a semi-truck driver that kept driving into heaven, loading up and bringing back warehouses of God's words and gifts and distributing them to the multitudes. She'll know nothing of this book until she reads these lines. But perhaps one of the more surreal moments of the week came when an auditor of the Bethel school who had never spoken to me before told me that the Lord had awakened her at 3 AM that morning with a word from the Psalms that she was supposed to give to me. It was more powerful and meaningful to me than she could have imagined. One of the main reasons that I recalled the manuscript was to include her words as the foreword of this book.

While these things may sound a bit beyond your experiences, they are all a daily part of the incredible Kingdom life that the Lord has directed me to write about in this book. I pray that the Holy Spirit will guide you and comfort you through the next chapter. You are likely to read things that might possibly offend you. Please believe me that it is the furthest thing from my heart to do, but I must tell you the truth of what the Holy Spirit is revealing to us in this apostolic season.

The Kingdom message is ushering in the greatest revival that mankind has ever seen. It is sweeping the globe, and it is unlike anything that the Earth has witnessed since the ministry of Jesus. The Lord is opening up the scripture to His bride and calling her to present herself into the Kingdom. She is to be whole with no division and wholesome with no bitterness.

He that hath ears to hear, let him hear - Matthew 11:15 (King James Version).

Chapter 13
A Time to Unlearn

To everything there is a season, and a time to every purpose under the Heaven.

Ecclesiastes 3:1 (King James Version)

Some of the things in this chapter go against the grain of everything that we have ever been taught about what a Christian is. That's one of the reasons that this book starts off with the questions "have you ever been wrong? Have you ever thought that something was true and found out that it just wasn't?" Herein are some Kingdom truths that blow away the erroneous strongholds that the religious churches have always taught.

I've decided to just dive headfirst into this chapter starting off with a big one... the topic of sin. The main reason for starting with this behemoth is that the church culture has allowed sin to be a stumbling block. They have then gathered all the stumbling blocks to build a wall. The wall effectively keeps out the world, but it simultaneously walls in the believer. I am suddenly reminded of the insidious Edgar Allan Poe story entitled "The Casque of Amontillado". The story concerns the murderous revenge that is perpetrated upon Fortunato by the story's narrator Montresor, when the former is lured into his own immurement.

Contrary to religious teachings, living a Christian life has nothing to do with trying not to sin.

"And we're off..."

As a matter of fact, it has nothing to do with sin at all, because God no longer sees the sin in our life once we accept His cleansing. Paul attempts to explain this to the Romans in chapters 5, 6 and 7. He does this by continually juxtaposing his newfound freedom and life in Christ with his previous life of trying to live a righteous life under the law. Trying to live a good and moral life without Christ is impossible, and Paul does a good job of explaining that. The problems arise when carnal man reads Paul's letter as if, even after Jesus had set him free from sin, he was writing as one who was still a slave to sin. This is absolutely not the case, and Paul makes it abundantly clear in those three chapters, if we would only allow the Holy Spirit to lead us through its reading.

Following Christ has nothing to do with trying not to sin; but is all about a love relationship with Him. If we would just focus on the relationship, the sin would take care of itself. Of course, this doesn't mean that we can forgo pursuing a relationship but still have a free pass to sin. God will not be mocked. We are judged according to our heart. If our heart is seeking after Him, we have nothing to worry about, and it's an evil, false doctrine that tells us that we need to keep repenting for our sins week after week.

The Christian life, as it has been taught for the past several hundred years, has been so distorted and perverted by religion that it truly bears little resemblance to anything that God ever had in mind for His bride. Listen to how Paul describes what Jesus is looking for. *Husbands, love your wives, even as Christ also loved the church, and gave himself for it; that he might sanctify and cleanse it with the washing of water by the word, That he might present it to himself a glorious church, not having spot, or wrinkle, or any such thing; but that it should be holy and without blemish. So ought men to love their wives as their own bodies. He that loveth his wife loveth himself. For no man ever yet hated his own flesh; but nourisheth and cherisheth it, even as the Lord the church: For we are members of his body, of his flesh, and of his bones* - Ephesians 5:25-30 (King James Version).

Therefore, I'm going to refer to the life that we were intended to have as Kingdom life, and compare and contrast it with the religious Christian dogma.

The differences in the religious Christian and the Kingdom Christian are striking, and start showing up even before the walk begins. This is because the religious Christian has always been taught that the first step is getting into church (that's the reason that you might often get invited to church. This is one of the only ways that Christians have been taught how to witness. They believe that once they have brought someone to church, it's then the preacher's job to deliver a fiery message that will literally scare the hell out of the sinner, put them under conviction, and send them running to the altar.) The other witnessing method that they employ is only used by a handful of the bold. This is where the individual tries to explain that "You are lost and bound for hell, but Jesus will save you if you just turn to Him."

Even among these bold witnesses, there are varying levels and degrees of how much each individual feels comfortable in telling someone that they need to repent and change their ways. The most timid don't even want to confront a person, but they've always been taught that they should witness, so they do this by leaving Jack Chick tracts in public restrooms. Some of the more bold ones might even mess up your lunch break with something like: "You don't really need all those beers for the big game tonight! What you're really thirsty for is God in your life." There are those that go door to door to let you know that you're bound for hell, some that lug a heavy cross down the highway, and even a few scary ones that stand on street corners and scream at you, Bible in hand.

Please keep in mind that the vast majority of these religious Christians are not bad people. As a matter of fact, most of them try to live a good life and think of themselves as good people. Some of them may even be trying to disassociate themselves with the trappings of religion, but just haven't yet found a way. They only do the things that they do because that's all they know. That's what they've been taught to do, and they want to try to do what they've been told is the right thing. Christians and non-Christians alike can recognize most all of the above scenarios, because they've seen it throughout their entire life. Let's pause for a moment for another task. I would like you to read the above paragraphs again about Christian witnessing. Read slowly and check it with the spirit that is within you. Now that you see it printed in black-and-white, and once you go back and reread it... doesn't it feel a little bit icky?

The first time that you skimmed over it, you might have been saying to yourself "Well self, that's correct... that's how you should witness." My question is... Have you ever been wrong about anything? At a glance, the scenarios sound like they're correct because these things have been promulgated by the church for centuries. We have grown up with them, so they seem natural. It's like growing up in the ethnicity that you grew up in. It's in you; it's a part of you.

Here is something for you to think about. Where does this stuff come from? If these things are correct, surely they are mentioned in the Bible somewhere. Surely Jesus preached at least one message that put people under conviction. You mean He didn't? Not only did He not, but the word *conviction* isn't even in the Bible. Then, if people never come under conviction; they will never repent! How will they ever get saved? Most people are amazed to find out that what they have always been taught about Christianity is nowhere to be found in the Bible. Nowhere does it even hint at conviction leading to repentance. In fact, in the second chapter of Romans, Paul writes: *Do you show contempt for the riches of His kindness, tolerance and patience? Don't you realize that it is God's kindness and goodness that leads you to repentance?*

His Kindness and goodness lead to repentance? You don't even have to go to the Scriptures to know that Jesus went around the land doing good things. He healed the sick. He raised the dead. He cleansed the leper, unstopped the deaf ears and opened the blind eyes. He never asked anyone their heritage or religious affiliation. He never asked them about the condition of their hearts. He never judged them. He never preached hellfire and brimstone at them. He simply met their physical needs with miracles, healings, goodness and kindness poured out from the Father. The miracles and the signs and the wonders are what drew people to Jesus. In the book of John, Jesus even states: ... *even if you do not believe my words, believe the miracles* - John 10:38.

Some may try to convince you that Jesus couldn't preach conviction, because the Holy Spirit had not yet been poured out, and wouldn't be until after His death. This just simply isn't the case, however. Jesus taught us everything that we need to know in order to minister the Kingdom of God to others. If you follow the above logic, how could one become born again, or be born of the Spirit before Jesus died and the Holy Spirit was poured out? Yet Jesus clearly taught Nicodemus that he must be born again of the Spirit. If Jesus could not have taught conviction before His death and before the Spirit had been poured out, then He could not have taught being born again of the Spirit for the same reason. *Jesus answered, Verily,*

verily, I say unto thee, Except a man be born of water and of the Spirit, he cannot enter into the kingdom of God - John 3:5 (King James Version).

The Bible teaches that the mystery of Christ is that he was 100% man, and yet simultaneously 100% God. He wasn't a hybrid or a mixture of the two. Yet, when He dealt with humankind, it was strictly as a human. He didn't come to Earth and perform signs, miracles, wonders and healings as God. God didn't need to come to Earth to create miracles. He could have done that from the Heavenly realm. Jesus performed miracles in order to show people what a man who was in relationship with God could accomplish. If he had performed miracles as God, then we, as mere humans, would have no hope of even coming close to the works of God. But as a man in relationship with God, Jesus said *"Verily, verily, I say unto you, He that believeth on me, the works that I do shall he do also; and greater works than these shall he do; because I go unto my Father. And whatsoever ye shall ask in my name, that will I do, that the Father may be glorified in the Son"* - John 14:12 (King James Version).

One highway of false doctrine entering the church is the fact that many pastors, preachers, evangelists and teachers believe that they must convey themselves as being omniscient, or knowing everything. The prophet Daniel had visions that he wrote down, and then said "I don't understand it". Even though the apostle Thomas didn't comprehend, or at first even believe the resurrection, even though the disciples had to ask Jesus for explanations to his parables, today's preachers have self-imposed pressures to have complete and accurate understandings of the entirety of the Scriptures. The Bible doesn't record even one teacher among the Pharisees and Sadducees, other than Jesus, that had a proper understanding of the Scriptures. Obviously, the direct disciples that had been coming into the church did not have a proper understanding of the operations and applications, or we would have no New Testament. The New Testament is comprised of letters from the apostles written to those who were teaching, to explain their mistakes and misunderstandings.

With so many of the teachers of the early church willing to admit a lack of understanding, and willing to accept guidance from those who had encountered it firsthand, why do so many of today's teachers have an attitude or air about them as to their complete and total understanding of the Scripture? If there is something that they truly don't understand; some will go so far as to try to bluff their way through an explanation rather than just admitting that they don't have the answers. As the congregation sees that the pastor always has an answer, the pastor's ego grows unchecked; because whether it is accurate or not, he always has an explanation of a biblical verse or principle. There is absolutely nothing wrong with a pastor claiming "I don't understand this passage"! I would a million to one rather hear this than to be sitting under someone who creates confusion by always having a readymade interpretation be it right or wrong. There are many things that we do not understand, and in some cases we never will in this life. Let's just start answering that we don't understand why some things happen in the manner in which they do, and leave it at that.

Another major teaching that we must unlearn concerns the Bible as a whole. One of the biggest causes of so many denominational divisions, and splits from the teachings of Christ is ironically due to reading the Bible. As you are most likely aware, the Bible was not written as a book, it is a collection of letters that were written by many different people. The people who truly changed the world are the disciples of Jesus, and those disciples whom they brought into the fold; and for decades they did so with no Bible. How were they able to do this? Many Christians have been trained that the only way in which we can know the word and will of God is to read about it in the Bible. Yet, there is something that the old covenant prophet Jeremiah dreamed about, and recorded in the 31st chapter of the book that bears his name. In the days of the Old Testament, when the house of Israel was under the Law of Moses, there were indeed written laws... 613 of them! But God spoke to Jeremiah in a dream, and showed him things that were to come under the new covenant:

"The time is coming," declares the LORD, "when I will make a new covenant with the house of Israel and with the house of Judah. It will not be like the covenant I made with their forefathers when I took them by the hand to lead them out of Egypt, because they broke my covenant, though I was a husband to them," declares the LORD.

"This is the covenant I will make with the house of Israel after that time," declares the LORD. "I will put my law in their minds and write it on their hearts. I will be their God, and they will be my people. No longer will a man teach his neighbor, or a man his brother, saying, 'Know the LORD,' because they will all know me, from the least of them to the greatest," declares the LORD. "For I will forgive their wickedness and will remember their sins no more."

There is a pharisaical, religious spirit in the world today, just like there was in the days of Jesus. Jesus never had a harsh word to say to a "sinner"; but to these people who like to play church, and go to all their churchly functions of the churchly cliques in churchly suits and dresses so that they seem churchly in the eyes of their neighbors, Jesus unleashed a mind crushing onslaught that still reverberates from the gates of hell to the stained-glass windows of the monumental cemeteries that they have built for themselves. It is these religious, and their forefathers, and their descendents who have used the Bible as a weapon. When they found this sword to be not quite so effective on the world, and found the enemy a little too intimidating to even pull it out of its sheath against, they started wielding it toward one another. There they found that *the word of God is quick, and powerful, and sharper than any twoedged sword, piercing even to the dividing asunder of soul and spirit.*

The original letters, now called the books of the Bible, were written under direct inspiration and supervision of the Holy Spirit. They were written to people who were filled with the Spirit, and who understood that you had to read the letters through the guidance of the Holy Spirit. Some of the letters are to the spirit man, and some are written to the heart. Few sentences in fewer books however, were written to the head... or to the intellect. Problems have always arisen when people who were not Spirit filled began reading the Bible only on an intellectual level.

Unless you read the Bible in spirit and in truth, you can become confused and easily led astray. Because of this, it's also an incorrect and harmful policy to tell the lost to start reading the Bible to learn more about God. That's exactly what you *don't* want them to do! It wasn't written to them! It will do nothing but confuse and divide them.

As people read the Bible with the carnal mind or simply on an intellectual level without filtering it through the Holy Spirit, they begin to misinterpret it. When another person reads it without guidance, they get a whole different interpretation. Once there are different interpretations, church culture dictates that one or both must leave. One will leave, start another church, and the pattern will continue.

Once we step into perfection, do you really believe that there will be arguing among people of various denominations about the exact interpretation of Scripture? Of course not. That is the desire of the Father right now... for us to step into perfection... for His Kingdom to completely fill the entire Earth. Obviously, we need to rightly divide the Word, but that can only be done through the guidance of the Holy Spirit. If people debate back and forth trying to convince one another of a particular interpretation of the Word, the best (or worst) that could ever be accomplished is to change somebody's mind. If your mind can be changed, then it can be changed again. We don't need an intellectual changing of the mind; we need a spiritual changing of the heart.

A sure sign of a religious spirit is arguing or debating the Word of God, or trying to convince or sway others to an opinion on an intellectual basis. The religious make such a big deal of every little minor detail of the Scripture until it becomes chains of legalism. There are those who claim that only the King James Version of the Bible can be read. There are others that say only the actual 1611 authorized King James Version can be read. Still others claim that this word or that word is not a correct translation from the original writings (none of which, by the way, still exist). Is this what Jesus died for? So that His followers could argue about words that others have written about Him? If you are truly pursuing a relationship with the Father with all of your heart, and are asking the Holy Spirit to guide you as you read the Word, do you really believe that God would allow you to be led astray because you're not reading a particular version of the Bible that was written in a particular language by a particular translator? And if so, who would want to spend eternity under such a tyrannical dictatorship in the first place?

I know that this might be shocking for some to read. Just bear with me for a moment and read the entire next paragraph. Truth be told, we no longer even need the Bible in order to know God and His heart. Throw it away! It is only words that were written by man, printed and distributed by man, and then continually argued by man. It has been wrongly interpreted from the moment it was written. It has been mistranslated, misused, misappropriated and misrepresented... why keep it?

Now, that was a good test to see if there is a religious spirit in you, or even the hint of one. Did you feel your hair standing on edge as you read? Was your face turning red? Was the anger beginning to boil inside of you? That anger is not of God. Remember, what God wants from you is a relationship. He will speak his laws into your mind and write his desires on your heart if you will truly seek after him. Even though I am sure to be misquoted by the religious, I am not advocating burning all the Bibles! I know that the men who wrote the original letters were doing so under influence of the Holy Spirit. I am only challenging you to think for yourself. A child and a parent automatically have a nurturing and loving relationship. You don't need to write a thousand page rule book on how you want to be treated, and require your child to memorize it in order for you to love him. There are parents that write down rules for their children. While there is nothing at all wrong with having a rulebook, wouldn't it break your heart if your children were more interested in picking apart every little minute detail about the punctuation of your book, and in arguing with each other about what you actually mean by a statement, rather than building a relationship with you?

Chapter 14
Gathering the Keys

By now, even though you might not realize it, you've obtained most of the keys that you're going to need to walk and live in the Kingdom. Remember in the Introduction that I told you that they were hanging on the words of this book? If you have been reading it in order, praying for guidance, and following the tasks completely; then you've already been gathering them as you've walked along the path.

You need the keys of identity. You need to know who you are in God, and you need to know who God is in you. These two keys of identity are important ones that have been stolen away. It's time that we reclaim them, and use them to open the first two locks of the door. The identity of God and His heart was revealed to you in the book that I had you read. If you didn't read it, then you have no idea what I'm talking about. If you decide not to read it, then you have no desire to *know* what I'm talking about. If you have no desire to *know* who God is, then the door will remain locked. The other identity key is *your* identity. Your true identity is not who *you* think that you are, but who *God* thinks that you are.

The third key is just as important, the key of worship. You cannot know God outside of worship. Did you ask yourself why this book title is *Seven Keys*, when only three are shown on the artwork? I'll get ahead of myself momentarily to answer that. The doorway into the Kingdom is called *Relationship*. There are three master keys that, if perfected, will unlock the door. If you know the true heart of God and live for it, if you know your true identity as God sees it and love and live it out, and if you know the heart of true worship and practice it constantly; then you already walk in love. Jesus said: *By this shall all men know that ye are my disciples, if ye have love one to another* - John 13:35 (King James Version). One good self analysis of your love is to read the *Love* verses from Corinthians, and replace the words "*Love is*" with the words "*I am*". It would read something like this:

I am patient, I am kind. I do not envy, I do not boast, I am not proud. I am not rude, I am not self-seeking, I am not easily angered, I keep no record of wrongs. I do not delight in evil but rejoice with the truth. I always protect, always trust, always hope, and always persevere. I never fail to walk in love - I Corinthians 13:4-8 (New International Version / edited by Pinky). If these two paragraphs describe you, then you may open the door and start living Kingdom. For the rest of us, it might be that we need to collect the remaining keys. You will also need to possess the key of self-control. You need to realize that you no longer have to be externally controlled by the rules and regulations that the religious world tries to pile on top of your head. You have been set free. If your heart is pure, and you follow Christ in love, there is no more sin in your life as far as God is concerned. Will you mess up? Probably. Do you need to beg for forgiveness? Nope… God chooses to no longer see it. Asking for forgiveness for something that is no longer there is not only futile, but counterproductive. Instead of asking for forgiveness, offer praise. Crawl up into His lap, throw your arms around His neck, and tell Him how much you love Him.

The fifth key is communication. By now, you know some of the ways in which you can communicate with God that truly work. Besides worship, you now know that you can pray and actually see the result or the answer. Is it God's will to heal or to hurt? Is it God's will to deliver or to bind in chains? Is it God's will to save or to turn His back on the lost? Is it God's will to set free or to lock up? Is it God's will to give you the desires of your heart or to deny your needs? You see, you already *know* the will of God. Therefore, never, never, never again pray "If it be thy will…" Praying those words is another attack from the enemy to cause us to doubt God and His abilities. Remember, the most devastatingly deceptive lie from chapter ten?

Satan will tell you "But didn't Jesus pray… *Father, if thou be willing, remove this cup from me: nevertheless not my will, but thine, be done* - Luke 22:42 (King James Version)?" The right scripture quoted at the wrong time becomes a lie. Jesus knew the will of the Father perfectly well. His prayer was not one of admitting that He didn't know the will of the Father, but a request for the Father to consider changing His mind. Jesus never prayed "Father, if thou be willing, heal this leper", or "give this man sight", or "let this one hear again", or even "raise this one from the dead". Jesus knew the will of the Father, and knew that He was living under an open Heaven. He didn't have to say "What should I do, Daddy?"

Jesus simply thanked the Father (for the benefit of the onlookers), and then called on the dead to arise. *Then they took away the stone from the place where the dead was laid. And Jesus lifted up his eyes, and said, Father, I thank thee that thou hast heard me. And I knew that thou hearest me always: but because of the people which stand by I said it, that they may believe that thou hast sent me. And when he thus had spoken, he cried with a loud voice, Lazarus, come forth. And he that was dead came forth, bound hand and foot with grave clothes, and his face was bound about with a napkin. Jesus saith unto them, Loose him, and let him go* - John 11:41-44 (King James Version). Just like Jesus, you know God's will. By using the phrase "If it be thy will…" when you pray, you cop out so you won't feel bad in front of your friends in case the answer doesn't come right away. "Oh well… must not have been His will" you comfort your ego. How much faith does it take to say "God, heal her… if you want to."?

The key that you received in the previous chapter is the key of understanding of a Kingdom culture versus a church culture. You need to always keep in mind that going to church, in the traditional sense, has not prepared us for Kingdom living. As a matter of fact, it has confused us to the point that it becomes difficult to understand the truths that Jesus tried to impart because they rarely if ever follow alongside with church culture.

A church culture is about controlling you.

A Kingdom culture is about self control.

A church culture is about rules and regulations.

A Kingdom culture is about truth and love.

A church culture is about trying to live a good life and trying not to sin.

A Kingdom culture is about pursuing the heart of the Father, and therein accomplishing both.

A church culture is about debating or arguing scripture.

A Kingdom culture is about following your heart through the guidance of the Holy Spirit.

A church culture is about gathering with those who believe the same way that you do.

A Kingdom culture is about gathering with those who love the Lord the same way that you do.

A church culture is about asking someone what would happen to them if they died tonight, and trying to talk with them to steer them toward the Lord through witnessing.

A Kingdom culture is about asking someone if they have any needs that you could help them with, be it physical, mental or spiritual; allowing them to see God's kindness

A church culture is about trying to get someone to come to church with you so that they might get under conviction and come to repentance.

A Kingdom culture is about delivering the power and goodness of God into someone's life so that they might see how much God loves them, and come to repentance.

A church culture is about God ruling from the throne of Heaven with an iron rod.

A Kingdom culture is about God ruling from the throne of your heart with open arms.

A church culture is about John 3:16.

A Kingdom culture is about John 3:16… and 17.

A church culture is about Jesus dying on the cross for your sins.

A Kingdom culture is about Jesus resurrecting to give you a joyous, abundant and powerful life.

I pray the Holy Spirit to strengthen you and guide you away from the church culture created by man, and into the Kingdom culture created for you by the Creator.

Chapter 15
The final key that Opens the Door

The seventh key is power. Don't worry, I didn't just blurt out the end of the book too soon. In fact, there is so much involved in understanding power, and so much to understand, that this chapter will be one of the most important, and the most in-depth chapters of all. This chapter will not only explain how everything comes together, but reveal exactly what the Kingdom is, how you live and operate in it, how its truths turn the traditional teachings of Christianity upside down, and how your Christian walk is getting ready to explode into a Disneyland-like adventure that you have never before imagined.

The best way that I can describe it is this: Think about everything that you know about church; think about everything that you've always been taught about what a Christian is, then know that living the true Christian life in a Kingdom culture is just the opposite. Where there were rules... they have melted away into love. Where there was order, it has dissolved... not into chaos; but into openings and invitations of the Holy Spirit. Where there was boredom of tradition, there is excitement of discovery. Where there was a constant awareness of sin, there is complete freedom in redemption. Where there was a notion of being weak and powerless, there is an explosion of vitality. Where there was a begrudging fulfilling of duties and requirements, there is a free-flowing river that we can dive into and float down. Where there was work to be done, there is fun to be experienced. Where there was pious living, there is gaiety. Where there was hardship and need, there is plenty. Where there was sickness, there is health. Where there was the burden of prayer, there is the joy of thanksgiving. Where there was the fear of witnessing to the lost, there is the excitement of having the lost ask you how they could receive what you have. Where there was the need to get away from Christians in order to have fun, there is the freedom to be exactly who you are without the fear of condemnation. Believe me this list could go on to become a book of its own. Instead of that, before you read the next paragraph, read the first sentence of this paragraph again.

Before we tie Kingdom life all together with a pretty bow, we need to discuss the final key of power. After the death of Jesus, and after His resurrection, He appeared to his disciples for a period of 40 days. He taught them many things during this time, and one of those things is this: *"But ye shall receive power, after that the Holy Ghost is come upon you: and ye shall be witnesses unto me both in Jerusalem, and in all Judaea, and in Samaria, and unto the uttermost part of the Earth"* - Acts 1:8 (King James Version). So the Holy Ghost was to be given, and the disciples were to receive power. What kind of power, exactly, are we talking about? That could best be answered by looking at what happened to the disciples, and what power they were given once they received the Holy Spirit. To begin with, they had disbanded. They thought that their lives were over after the crucifixion. They were scared and in hiding. What kind of power could have turned them from unbelieving cowards into fearless and mighty men of valor?

And when the day of Pentecost was fully come, they were all with one accord in one place. And suddenly there came a sound from Heaven as of a rushing mighty wind, and it filled all the house where they were sitting. And there appeared unto them cloven tongues like as of fire, and it sat upon each of them. And they were all filled with the Holy Ghost, and began to speak with other tongues, as the Spirit gave them utterance - Acts 2:1-4 (King James Version).

Now Peter and John were going up to the temple at three o'clock in the afternoon, when a certain man crippled from his birth was being carried along, who was laid each day at that gate of the temple (which is called Beautiful), so that he might beg for charitable gifts from those who entered the temple. So when he saw Peter and John about to go into the temple, he asked them to give him a gift. And Peter directed his gaze intently at him, and so did John, and said, Look at us! And the man paid attention to them, expecting that he was going to get something from them. But Peter said, Silver and gold I do not have; but what I do have, that I give to you: in the name of Jesus Christ of Nazareth, walk! Then he took hold of the man's right hand with a firm grip and raised him up. And at once his feet and ankle bones became strong and steady, and leaping forth he stood and began to walk, and he went into the temple with them, walking and leaping and praising God. And all the people saw him walking about and praising God, and they recognized him as the man who usually sat begging for alms at the Beautiful Gate of the temple; and they were filled with wonder and amazement and bewilderment over what had occurred to him. Now while he firmly clung to Peter and John, all the people in utmost amazement ran together and crowded around them in the covered porch called Solomon's Porch. And Peter, seeing it, answered the people, you men of Israel, why are you so surprised and wondering at this? Why do you keep staring at us, as though by our own individual power or piety we had made this man able to walk? - Acts 3:1-12 (Amplified Bible).

In these Scriptures are two demonstrations of power that the disciples received. There are many, many, more; but for the sake of our discussion, these two will suffice. Before we discuss these two demonstrations of power, we need to talk about the biases that might exist in your life concerning these powers. I wrote earlier in this book about preachers and teachers who felt obligated to know every answer. Of course, no man knows all of the answers, and some answers are known only to God. One of the major problems with teachers thinking along the line that he or she must supply every question with some type of answer is that many times when the answer is not truly known, the answer that is given is simply incorrect.

That is one of the major reasons that you might hear so many inconsistencies from one preacher to the next. If you want a true understanding of what the Lord has for you, be willing to lay down everything that you've been taught by man if it cannot be verified while reading the Scriptures with the guidance of the Holy Spirit. I find it truly amazing that the people who are the most bulldogged determined to argue their point or interpretation of the Scripture are those who have never truly prayed for the guidance of the Holy Spirit to help them read and understand it. The ones who argue their point the most are those who have head knowledge of a particular scripture, but lack the heart encounter of it. These are those who have only been told what the Scripture means by a friend, pastor, book or seminary institution.

For now, I implore you to set aside your doctrinal training and learned beliefs, and look to the Scripture for the truth. When teachers are asked why their teachings or experience doesn't line up with scriptures, they feel obligated to give some type of answer, even if it's wrong. Because of this, some teachers say that the Holy Spirit was poured out upon the original disciples and was not again given, or that it is still given without power. The Scripture says: *Peter replied, "Repent and be baptized, every one of you, in the name of Jesus Christ for the forgiveness of your sins. And you will receive the gift of the Holy Spirit. The promise is for you and your children and for all who are far off—for all whom the Lord our God will call." - Acts 2:38-30* (New International Version).

Coming from my own encounters, I can state unequivocally that there is indeed an outpouring of the Holy Spirit that is (or at least _can be_) a completely separate experience from that of accepting the Lord into your life and being baptized in water. While an encounter is a greater teacher then learned knowledge, our encounters still need to line up with what the Scripture says. Does the Scripture teach that there is a separate experience of being baptized in the Holy Spirit from that of accepting the Lord into ones heart?

While Apollos was at Corinth, Paul took the road through the interior and arrived at Ephesus. There he found some disciples and asked them, "Did you receive the Holy Spirit when (or after) you believed?" They answered, "No, we have not even heard that there is a Holy Spirit." So Paul asked, "Then what baptism did you receive?" "John's baptism," they replied. Paul said, "John's baptism was a baptism of repentance. He told the people to believe in the one coming after him, that is, in Jesus." On hearing this, they were baptized in the name of the Lord Jesus. When Paul placed his hands on them, the Holy Spirit came on them, and they spoke in tongues and prophesied. There were about twelve men in all - Acts 19:1-7 (New International Version).

There are two things that I would want you to garner from this example. Both of these things will help you on your journey of learning how to think rather than being told what to think. The first thing is this: It is nearly impossible to convince someone that something is not real after they have already experienced the reality of it. For instance, I have seen the Cincinnati Reds professional baseball team play baseball many times, over a period of several years, in a field that used to be called Redland. The field is no longer in existence. You might inform me that the Cincinnati ballclub plays in a Stadium called Cinergy Field, and that before that it was called Riverfront Stadium. You might tell me that prior to the 1970 Riverfront Stadium, the team played in Crosley field that was built in the early 1900s... so I surely must be mistaken. Remember, however, I had the encounters.

No amount of someone else's head knowledge or persuasion can take away my experience. Encounters are better than knowledge. It's no longer good enough to simply *know* the Lord; He's calling you to encounters with Him. Do you simply *know* your husband or wife? Or have you had experience with them. How about your children? When asked about your child, would you simply state "I know him or her"? The Lord desires to be closer to us than our family. He longs to be more intimate with us than any human being could possibly be; yet most of us are comfortable with our testimony simply being "I know the Lord".

The second thing that I would have you to keep in mind is this: it is all but impossible to prove a negative. For instance, you might tell me that you have never been arrested, but if I ask you to prove that to me, how would you do it? This is why I have always said that there is no such thing as an intelligent atheist. Why? Because the atheist's claim is that there is no God. An intelligent person quickly realizes the abstract negative. Could there be any type of higher intelligence or creative being on any planet within any galaxy of any universe or beyond that I might choose to refer to as God? While there might not be a clear cut method of proving this existence to the satisfaction of all, there is definitely no way to prove the negative or the nonexistence. If one cannot intelligently or experientially show that there is proof of a nonexistence of God, then how can one claim nonexistence? If one cannot claim the nonexistence of God, then one cannot intelligently claim to be an atheist.

Because it is outside of their realm of experience, encounter and/or training, there are those teachers that explain away tongues and healings as no longer existing. Of course there are many more gifts that the Holy Spirit empowers us with, but I have chosen these two for our topic simply because of their chronological order. Other than at the end of the second Chapter of Acts where it generally states that many wonders and miraculous signs were done, the gifts of tongues and the healing of the lame man are, chronologically speaking, the first two recordings of the power of the Holy Spirit operating in a believer. Some teachers and preachers claim that tongues served its purpose of allowing everyone to hear the gospel in their own language, and then it was done away with. If that is the case, why does it keep appearing throughout the entirety of the Scriptures with no reference to others understanding the language? More importantly, when was it done away with? It was definitely not within the lifetimes of the early disciples or the decades to follow that are recorded in Scripture. I tend to think that if the Bible gives no cutoff date and no hint of a future cutoff date, then there has most likely not been a cutoff. I especially feel this way when I see tongues being properly used in the daily lives of believers today. No intellectual debate of tongues can be a greater teacher than experiencing it for yourself.

What about healing? Why were the disciples given the ability to heal through the Holy Spirit? Was it to heal people who were in need of healing? Was it a testimony? Was it for God to show Himself in His goodness and kindness so that men could see it and come to repentance? Was it a combination of all of these and more? Some preachers claim that it no longer exists, because that is what they have been taught in seminary. What sense does that make? Are there not people in today's world who need healing and need to be saved through witnessing the goodness and kindness of God? Let me ask you this: you may or may not know how difficult it is to ask somebody if they have accepted the Lord, and if they know beyond a shadow of a doubt that they are on their way to Heaven. Regardless of how they answer, you always feel like the underdog trying to muster the courage to witness Jesus to someone who has no interest.

Now, suppose that you walk up to a young lady in a wheelchair and asked her if you could pray for her. When she says yes, you lay your hand on her leg and say "In the name of Jesus of Nazareth, rise up and walk". If the lady stands up and walks, you are going to hear screams and gasps and mumblings, and a crowd is going to gather around you and start asking you how they could get healed and saved. This scenario is not make-believe. This is not a hopeful future event that we can look forward to someday in the next world... these things are happening before our very eyes. They are happening all over the world. I have seen it with my own eyes, and I have seen it in my own life. Due to a devastating 2007 accident, my injured leg became necrotic, and the necrosis could not be reversed. For weeks on end, I spent two hours each day in a state-of-the-art hyperbaric oxygen dive chamber with no good news, and no reversal of the necrosis. I was then sent out of state to a Harvard trained micro-surgeon who had completed fellowship at M.D. Anderson. In other words, this doctor was the best of the best; and he told me that the best I could hope for was to be permanently disfigured and walk with assistance, or at least a limp. That was the best case scenario. What was the worst? He told me to consider the real possibility that I might lose the leg. Before I went into the potentially eight hour-long reconstructive surgery that might give me a 50-50 chance of keeping my leg, I went to my fellowship and had them lay hands on me and pray for my leg. To make a long story short, the surgeon came out of the operating room in minutes instead of hours, and claims to have never seen anything like my situation. It seemed that all of the destroyed, necrotic and missing tissue had grown back overnight. The only surgery that this highly trained micro-surgeon had to perform was a simple skin graft over the wound, which any surgeon could have completed. In a follow-up visit to an orthopedic surgeon, he claimed my situation to be a miracle.

In the church culture, there is always at least that one story of how God performed something amazing years ago. It's repeated every so often to encourage the church goers, but we are living in a new move and outpouring of God, my friend. I see the miraculous every week. I have traveled to Kingdom minded gatherings throughout the United States, and I have seen so many hundreds of healings that I lost track long ago. I have seen gold dust appear on the hands of my family. I've witnessed a physical, dense glory cloud hovering over the entire audience for ten minutes... inside! I've seen feathers floating down from Heaven (inside buildings), gold teeth appear in mouths where there were none, and surgically inserted metal in arms, legs, necks and backs melt away into bone just to name a handful. I myself was lying in the operating room in 2010 to have a kidney stone removed that was too large to pass. The X-ray of the huge stone hung at one end of the OR, but I prophesized to the attending anesthesiologist that the stone had disintegrated before the procedure could be performed. When extracorporeal shock wave lithotripsy could not locate the stone after an hour, I was wheeled out of the OR and sent for more X-rays. They revealed nothing. Two more sets of magnetic resonance imaging over the next week revealed nothing. The stone had been rolled away.

God's Favor Shines Down

Since you can't imagine a place where He isn't, you might as well imagine Him with you. - Bill Johnson

This place, Bethel Church, has been such an amazing avenue for me to become better equipped for ministry. The Lord is truly pouring out His spirit upon Bethel. I have been fortunate to receive impartations from many of their mighty warriors of God.

One thing that I really find inspiring there are the prayers before an offering. I would like to share one with you now, and it is my prayer that these declarations become true for you.

— Lissa / Bethel Church, Redding, California

Proverbs 18:21 says that death and life are in the power of the tongue, so Jesus:

We are believing You for:
Heaven opened, Earth Invaded
Storehouses unlocked, and Miracles created;
Dreams and Visions, Angelic Visitations
Declarations, Visitations, and Divine Manifestations,
Anointing, Gifting, and Calls,
Positions, and promotions,
Provisions and Resources,
to go to the nations;
Souls and more souls,
from every generations,
Saved and set free,
Carrying Kingdom revelation!

Thank You, Father, that as I join my value system to Yours, You will shower FAVOR, BLESSINGS and INCREASE upon me so I have more than enough to co-labor with Heaven and see JESUS get His FULL REWARD. Hallelujah!!!!!!

Available at www.ibethel.org/site/offering-readings

This image may be freely downloaded for personal use at www.kingdomcultureministries.org

Epilogue

These things of which you have been reading are not just happening in my life or around me, they are happening all over the world. People are being saved around the world by the thousands because of the goodness and kindness of God in demonstrating the power of the Holy Spirit through signs, wonders, miracles and healings. There are many ways to allow God to start working miracles through you through the power of the Holy Spirit. One fun, fascinating and powerful way is called a Treasure Hunt. This is a term and concept that God revealed through Pastor Kevin Dedmon that is changing the world in the ways of ministry. Kevin is a history maker and a world changer. I sat in on one of his classes and went out on one of his treasure hunts a few years ago at the Bethel school BSSM in Redding California, and I was amazed. God is truly working wonders through this simple witnessing tool. People are being healed and brought to salvation through the goodness and kindness of God.

How many healings are we now seeing on treasure hunts? What kind of miracles are we witnessing? Trust me, simply listing them (with no other information) would create a list that this book could not contain. I will however, list one powerful life-changing event. On May 22, 2010, I was in Cleveland, Ohio for Jesus Culture 2010 at the Mason Arts Center. We were out in the city with treasure hunt teams and saw healings, miracles, and salvation that I hate to sound so matter-of-fact about... it's always exciting to see the work of God, but these things are now routine, daily occurrences! Not so in Cleveland, as one of our teams came back to report a resurrection! A child had died by drowning, and resuscitation attempts had failed. A member of the team laid her hands on the deceased, and in Jesus' name spoke life back into the child, who came to life at those words. EMS quickly loaded the now alive child into an ambulance and rushed to the ER. Follow-up calls to the hospital verified that the child was released with a clean bill of health.

Human logic and church culture nature might have a hard time with this one. They will come up with a laundry list of reasons of why this couldn't have occurred, and will offer explanation of what *really* happened. Will you listen to head-knowledge trying to prove a negative, or will you accept the true testimony of an eye-witness? I will never be offended about *what* you think about me, my testimonies, or the contents of this book. I was never concerned with *what* you thought in the first place; only with *how* you think. If you walk away from this book thinking differently about church, God, Christianity and/or relationships and identity, then the work that the Holy Spirit has commissioned of me has been accomplished.

It's high time for another task. I would like you to go to ibethel.org, Amazon.com or your favorite bookstore, and order a book called <u>The Ultimate Treasure Hunt</u> by Kevin Dedmon. If you are able, do so right now while it's still fresh in your mind, as this powerful book will forever change the way you witness to others. There is a revival going on all around you. It's time that you become a part of it. Kevin's book will take you by the hand and guide you through this incredible yet simple process in which God is manifesting Himself. One stalwart opposition that the religious have against the current world-wide revival is the statement "God doesn't work that way". Keep in mind that the Jews were adamantly seeking their Messiah, so how could they possibly have missed Jesus? Because of the stalwart opposition that the religious had against the move of God and the revival that was taking place at that time. The opposition was summarized in the statement "God doesn't work that way". Don't miss Jesus because of the clamor of the religious. Don't be left out of the glorious life that He has prepared for you. Don't listen to somebody trying to prove a negative.

The spirit of religion is the most evil and powerful tools of the enemy. It is incredibly difficult to break free of; but fortunately it's easy to spot. If you are in a church or fellowship where there is gossip, you will find it there. If you hear hatred or negativity being spoken about anyone, you are witnessing it. I know the authority by which I've written this book, and I know the hearts of the writers of the books that I've recommended. The spirit of religion will take a firm stance against all of these. The only thing that Jesus spoke out against was the spirit of religion. That evil spirit, however, will speak out against other churches, sinful lifestyles, Godless cities, ministers of the Gospel, new revivals or movements of God, and the list continues ad nauseam.

Not every minister who once or twice speaks negatively about people, places or things is under attack from a religious spirit; they might only need encouragement into the more perfect ways of love that God has for those things that He created. There are those however, that constantly spew forth bitterness and unkindness and negativity. While I'm never one to encourage a brother or sister to leave the place where God has planted them, if you are sitting under such teachings, you need to leave immediately unless you are already living a Kingdom lifestyle, and are sure that God has planted you in this place to bring about His will.

It makes no difference whether you claim yourself a Baptist, Catholic, Pentecostal, or Jew. If you are not filled with the Holy Spirit, then you are missing out on an incredible lifestyle that God has in mind for you. Some denominations try to make various gifts of the Spirit into matters of salvation. They are not in the least. Salvation is a separate issue. Once you accept Christ, however, He wants to shower you with gifts and blessings. He wants you to laugh and be full of joy. He wants you to have the things that you want, be who you want to be, do what you want to do, and have supernatural power. You won't go to hell for not operating in the gifts and power that He wants to give you. Those things are simply to help you while you remain here on Earth, and to aid you in furthering His Kingdom.

Don't listen to those who tell you that gifts like tongues and healings are no longer in operation. Instead, trust someone who has seen them happen. Trust someone who uses them every day. First of all, find a group of believers that can lay hands on you and pray for you to receive the Holy Spirit, or if you have already received the Holy Spirit, let them pray for you to receive the gift of tongues. Not only will this miraculous event open you up into the world of God's supernatural lifestyle, but it will be concrete evidence to you that God still does work in this manner.

Operating outside of what is natural to us (such as tongues or healings) is referred to as the supernatural. Supernatural events are any of God's workings. They are natural to Him. Only to us do they become supernatural. The devil has perverted the word to the point that, sadly, most Christians think of it as an anti-Christian term. Nothing could be further from the truth. If we could do all of the works of God, they would be natural to us.

As we cannot, we must refer to those works as supernatural. There is no negative connotation to the word. It has been used since the reformation to refer to the workings of God. Only for the last couple of centuries has it been used in association with ghosts and haunting as well. There is nothing that God has created that Satan hasn't tried to copy and pervert.

Once you receive the baptism of the Holy Spirit, or if you already have, read The Ultimate Treasure Hunt. It's time to start putting some of these works of God into practice. If you are happy with your home church, there is no reason to leave it. However, it is a must to seek out other Kingdom minded Christians for fellowship. The Door that you are opening to walk into the Kingdom is called *relationship*. Without entering the relationship door, there will be no entrance into the Kingdom. You first need the proper relationship with God. Most churches don't teach all of the intricacies of this relationship, because they themselves don't completely understand it. You also need a proper relationship with your family, pastor and brothers and sisters in Christ. Again, these are not the trainings that we have grown up in church receiving instruction in. My website might be helpful in aiding you to locate Kingdom minded fellowship and believers in your area that can help steer you toward Kingdom minded believers close to you. You can find Kingdom Culture Ministries at www.kingdomcultureministries. org. We also have speakers, teachers, prophetic ministry, healing and treasure hunt teams and leaders, and praise and worship teams that are willing and able to bring the supernatural to your church or fellowship.

Other good resources for you to look into are Bethel ministries that can be found at www.ibethel.org, and any book, CD, or teaching from the Bethel leaders such as Bill & Beni Johnson, Kris Vallotton, Danny Silk and others. There are also one year and two year schools of ministry located throughout the United States and around the world. More information can be found at the Bethel or Kingdom Culture websites.

The enemy has lied to you and stolen your identity for far too long! You are not a sinner saved by grace, but a priest or priestess of the Royal priesthood. You are not a pauper, but an heir to the throne... you are a child of the King! In your hands lie healing. In your words and works lies salvation. Through your actions the world can see the revelation of God on Earth. How can you sit there a moment longer, knowing your destiny yet not walking in it? Now is the time. Today is the day. This is the day that the Lord has made. Rise and be healed. Go forth and spread the good news that God is alive and on the throne. He's in a good mood, and longing to spread His kingdom throughout the Earth.

Finally, I want to leave you with a word of humility. As you begin to see healings, signs and wonders at your fingertips, you must not let it puff you up, as gifts are available to all believers. You must never become proud or boastful. Your gift is simply a free gift that God has given to you, and you are to give it away freely and never, ever allow anyone to put you on a pedestal because of it. Always remember the life that Jesus lived. The greatest man that ever walked the planet could have had the kings of the Earth falling at his feet; but he came humbly as a servant to all. Do not attempt to rise above your master.

Kingdom culture is a culture of honor and respect. Where there is humanity, there will be depravity. However there will also be pure hearts that are seeking God. We give honor to those hearts that have gone before us to pave the way. We honor the Catholic Church, as it is our roots. We honor the reformers for their teachings. We honor the different revivals and moves of God that have visited the Earth in times past. Their ceilings have become our floors. It's a church culture that will speak badly of another denomination, pastor, or Christian. Church culture focuses on the bad in others in order to justify itself. A Kingdom culture exalts, looks for and expects the good and honors it. Stop looking for the bad, and look for the good in people, places and things. Stop condemning and gossiping, and start honoring. Honor your elders in life as well as your elders in Christ. Honor your pastor and your church. If you give, you will receive.

As I am finishing this writing, I am just returning from a retreat at Chavada Ministries International All Nations Church, Healing and Revival Center in Fort Mill, South Carolina. The new building was wonderful, and the bathrooms were impeccable. However, as the days wore on, the sinks would become dirtier. They were so beautifully immaculate, that I wanted everyone to be able to walk in and see what I saw first thing in the morning. So, I made it my goal to clean the sink area each and every time that I went to the facility. I waited until the room was empty each time. No one ever saw me clean, nor did I ever tell anyone about it until now, as you read these words. I didn't do it to receive praise, as I made sure that no one saw. I didn't do it to be able to relate the story here, as this is but an afterthought. I did it because that's the way I live every day. I always try to bring honor. No matter where I am, I try to make things better for the next person. That's the heart of a servant. That's the heart that needs to beat in you. Now, go forth, through relationship, into the world of the supernatural. You have the keys...open the door.

Pinky Plays Pittsburgh

This photo is of the 2010 *Increase is Not an Option* conference at Pittsburgh's CCOP Covenant Church. Bishop Joseph L. Garlington's amazing legacy that was formerly All Nation's Church, is an incredible, multi-cultural experience like no other. The Love of God is powerful in this house, and the Bishop and his lovely bride, Pastor Barbara Williams Garlington, have grown a Kingdom culture of honor and love that is a joy to be in the presence of. My wife Lissa and I travel to churches around the country, and few can match the powerful anointing of this beautiful fellowship.

I want to bless and give honor to the Garlingtons, and my other friends and co-laborers in Christ at CCOP: Pastor Mike Silich, Pastor B.J. Bentley, Pastor Clarence Grant, Pastor Denise Graves, Pastor George Furlow, Jeanette Howard, Pastor Joe Jr. and Music Minister Jermaine Manor, and all the other Pastors and brothers and sisters that help to make CCOP such a beautiful experience. We look forward to being with you again.

This photo was taken by my wife as I was joining with the incredible CCOP praise and worship team. I can be seen in the background, but a camera has captured me on one of the big screens. Worshiping in the foreground is the Leadership of Bethel Church of Redding, California; Bill Johnson and Kris Vollotton. Bishop Garlington can barely be seen hidden behind Bill, along with his wife, Pastor Barbara.

Pinky / Pittsburgh COOP

This image may be freely downloaded for personal use at www.kingdomcultureministries.org

Addendum 1
Walking around the Kingdom

This addendum continues with some more New Testament Scriptures about the Kingdom, along with my commentary about them. While there are some important Scriptures and interesting commentary included here, it is a bit more academic than what I perceived the book chapters should be, and didn't flow well enough to be included as another chapter. For that reason, it has been added to this addendum section. Of course, there are many more Kingdom related Scriptures that didn't get included for one reason or another. The idea behind this addendum to chapter six is to allow the reader to see that Kingdom teachings are not just random scatterings, and are not just limited to one book of the Bible.

Matthew 24:14 *And this gospel of the kingdom shall be preached in all the world for a witness unto all nations; and then shall the end come.* This is Jesus speaking. He didn't say to preach hellfire and brimstone, or to place a church in every nation, or to scare people into salvation... He said to preach the gospel of the Kingdom to all nations. His commandment is now underway. After this shall be the end. Now is the hour to step into the Kingdom.

Matthew 25:1 *Then shall the Kingdom of Heaven be likened unto ten virgins, which took their lamps, and went forth to meet the bridegroom.* The implication that Jesus is making here is that the Kingdom of Heaven is already here... and going to meet the bridegroom. The church (the virgins) isn't on its way *into* the Kingdom... the Kingdom is on its way to the Bridegroom.

Matthew 25:14 *For the kingdom of Heaven is as a man travelling into a far country, who called his own servants, and delivered unto them his goods.*

This is the parable of the talents that compares Christians working in the Kingdom to servants who have been entrusted with money. Some Christians work with the gifts that the Kingdom has to offer, and some hide them away or say that they don't exist anymore. To those, even the gifts that they *do* have will be taken away. Another thing interesting to note is that Jesus sees these gifts as very valuable. Many Christians have the erroneous belief that a talent was a coin worth only a few cents; but comparing it to today's money, it was worth over $1000.00.

Matthew 25:34 *Then shall the King say unto them on his right hand, Come, ye blessed of my Father, inherit the Kingdom prepared for you from the foundation of the world:* At this time, we only have access to the Kingdom, or we only see parts of it, or we see through a glass darkly... but one day we will own it.

Matthew 26:29 *But I say unto you, I will not drink henceforth of this fruit of the vine, until that day when I drink it new with you in my Father's kingdom.* When did this happen? After Jesus died and was resurrected, He appeared to the disciples for a period of 40 days. He most probably ate and drank with them at that time. The first chapter of Acts records this event. In Acts 1:4, the Greek word *sunalizomenos,* is nearly always translated as "eating together". The very literal translation of the word is "sharing salt together." Both the Greeks and Romans used similar words to mean "having a meal together". Curiously enough, in this particular instance, the King James Version of the Bible translates this phrase as "gathered together" rather than "eating together". I know that there are those who have a different opinion than me... but I only serve one King... and his name isn't James. You may quote me on that.

Many of the Kingdom teachings throughout the Gospels are repeated, especially in the first three synoptic Gospels. For that reason, I am going to leave a lot of Kingdom verses out.

Mark Ch. 4 The entire fourth chapter of Mark is Jesus teaching about the Kingdom. The first twenty verses compare Kingdom teachings to the parable of the sower. Some will hear the Kingdom teaching and bear a lot of fruit with it. Others won't. It's a great chapter to read to learn about the Kingdom teachings. Jesus even states in the fourth chapter of Luke that the reason He was sent was to teach Kingdom messages. Luke 4:43 reads:

And he said unto them, I must preach the kingdom of God to other cities also: for therefore am I sent.

Luke 8:1 *And it came to pass afterward, that he went throughout every city and village, preaching and shewing the glad tidings of the kingdom of God: and the twelve were with him,* Jesus didn't just preach *about* the Kingdom, He showed it to the people through signs, miracles, wonders and healings.

Luke 9:60 *Jesus said unto him, Let the dead bury their dead: but go thou and preach the kingdom of God.* We are given a commission to do the same things that Jesus did.

Luke 9:62 *And Jesus said unto him, No man, having put his hand to the plough, and looking back, is fit for the kingdom of God.* Farmers know and understand this concept well. If you turn around while you plough to look back at where you came from… where you've already completed the work and moved on… you will get off the path, start going crooked and veer in the wrong direction. It doesn't mean that you are banned from farming by The Great Farm Association of America; it just means that unless you can quit looking back, you need to do something else besides plough. As most of us are no longer farmers, it might be a foreign phrase to understand the parable as saying: you need to stop teaching Kingdom principles if you can't stop looking back to the law and all of the crap that has been piled on top of you from denominationalism. There are others that can temporarily take the reins until your heart can completely get away from church culture and into the Kingdom.

Luke 10:9 *And heal the sick that are therein, and say unto them, the kingdom of God is come nigh unto you.* More stuff that we're supposed to be doing.

Luke 10:11 *Even the very dust of your city, which cleaveth on us, we do wipe off against you: notwithstanding be ye sure of this, that the kingdom of God is come nigh unto you.* They make it sound scary for those that reject Kingdom principles!

Luke 12:31 *But rather seek ye the kingdom of God; and all these things shall be added unto you.* The only thing that we are supposed to strive for is Kingdom and Kingdom teaching. All the other things will be added after we get that right.

Luke 16:16 *The law and the prophets were until John: since that time the kingdom of God is preached, and every man presseth into it.* Is it just me, or did Jesus just say that the Old Testament laws and prophets were only in effect until John the Baptist? Did He just say that, after John the Baptist, the message changed to Kingdom laws and principles?

Luke 17:20 *And when he was demanded of the Pharisees, when the kingdom of God should come, he answered them and said, The kingdom of God cometh not with observation:*

So, you're not going to physically see it happen. Think about this. If you are not able to see it happen, how will you know when it happens? Could it be happening right now, and you're simply not aware of it because you can't see it?

Luke 17:21 *Neither shall they say, Lo here! or, lo there! for, behold, the kingdom of God is within you.* This is the answer. You don't have to run to this place or to that place to look for it. If the Kingdom is within you, then wherever you are is where the Kingdom has the ability to invade our planet.

Luke 18:29-30 *And he said unto them, Verily I say unto you, There is no man that hath left house, or parents, or brethren, or wife, or children, for the kingdom of God's sake, Who shall not receive manifold more in this present time, and in the world to come life everlasting.* I have received, and continue to receive physical and monetary blessings enough to fill another book. A church culture discourages people from seeking blessings and rewards in this life, but Jesus clearly refers to them here.

Luke 19:11 *And as they heard these things, he added and spake a parable, because he was nigh to Jerusalem, and because they thought that the kingdom of God should immediately appear*

Luke 22:29 *And I appoint unto you a kingdom, as my Father hath appointed unto me; it was given to us.* He doesn't say "someday when you die you'll get to see it". He simply says I have appointed it to you.

Luke 22:30 *That ye may eat and drink at my table in my kingdom, and sit on thrones judging the twelve tribes of Israel.* Jesus has already stated that the Kingdom is not going to necessarily be a physical kingdom that we are going to see and move into. There is a physical kingdom, however that we will someday dwell in. To me, this verse speaks of that time. Otherwise, He would have us being judges at this time.

Luke 23:42 *And he said unto Jesus, Lord, remember me when thou comest into thy kingdom.* This is in reference to the thief on the cross speaking with Jesus. Again, this speaks to me of the actual, tangible domain of God, however, I would certainly not disagree with someone who saw this as strictly a spiritual kingdom.

John 3:3 *Jesus answered and said unto him, Verily, verily, I say unto thee, Except a man be born again, he cannot see the kingdom of God.* That's because the kingdom that Jesus is speaking of is a spiritual one that must be seen with spiritual eyes.

John 3:5 *Jesus answered, Verily, verily, I say unto thee, Except a man be born of water and of the Spirit, he cannot enter into the kingdom of God.* I see this as the spiritual kingdom that is all around us and within us... but it could certainly refer to the physical realm of God as well.

John 18:36 *Jesus answered, My kingdom is not of this world: if my kingdom were of this world, then would my servants fight, that I should not be delivered to the Jews: but now is my kingdom not from hence.* Jesus said many times throughout the Gospels that His Kingdom was here, or nigh, or close at hand. Is Jesus now saying that His Kingdom is not here all around us; but only in Heaven? Or is he saying that it is here on Earth all around us... but it's not of the material world; it's a spiritual world. Compare it to many other verses in the Bible that talks about not being of this world such as this verse in John: *If ye were of the world, the world would love his own: but because ye are not of the world, but I have chosen you out of the world, therefore the world hateth you* - John 15:19 (King James Version).

Addendum 2
A Message to the Religious World

This is yet another section which just didn't flow well, because it has no continuity with the Kingdom message of the love and goodness and righteousness of God. However, it is a very important message for the Christians and the churches that are locked into their religious denominationalism, and who are barring the doors into the Kingdom.

It is one thing if you have a heart for God and are truly seeking his guidance in your life. There are warriors standing in the gap reaching out to you with messages like the ones in this book. All He wants is a relationship. All He wants is your heart. You don't have to follow rules or regulations, or go to this church or that one; you need only give yourself to Him completely.

However, if you are thumbing your nose at this Kingdom message, and steering young or gullible Christians away from it, and keeping them locked up in a world of your rules and regulations; then the words of this addendum were written about you. This is a most important piece of writing for you to take note of, because I didn't write this message. I only interpreted the words and put them down to paper. This chapter was authored by your Creator.

The multitude of legalistic, religious teachers and preachers of this world only vomit up the letter of the Law as it was given to Moses. It's not that there's anything wrong with following the Ten Commandments... but all of the requirements of the Old Testament Law have already been fulfilled. *"Think not that I am come to destroy the law, or the prophets: I am not come to destroy, but to fulfill"* Jesus - Matthew 5:17 (King James Version). The problem with these self-righteous preachers is that they tell you that you have to follow the Ten Commandments; when they themselves don't even attempt to follow them! In other words, even though it's not a good idea to set your eyes on the Law and try to follow it, following the Law will certainly not hurt you. However, following the preacher that preaches it to you will. They keep piling the laws and the rules and regulations on top of you... but as it gets heavier and heavier; they won't lift a finger to help you out from underneath the burden.

Everything they do is for show. They love to wear fancy and expensive suits. They love to sit at the head of the dinner table, and on the streets, they glory in people calling them 'Father' and 'Reverend.'

If you teach or preach, don't allow people to put you up on a pedestal. The people that you are teaching are your equals in the Kingdom. It is only the least worthy in the Kingdom that tries to build himself up as something special. The truly greatest in the Kingdom will humble themselves with a servant's heart. While there's certainly nothing wrong with your children referring to you as their father, and there's nothing wrong with being a spiritual father, or mentor to new Christians, nobody on Earth should call themselves 'Father' as a title along with their name. This is because we all have one and the same Father in Heaven... and this is a descriptive title reserved for Him. Remember, God is only a descriptive title as well... it's not His name. Would you ever refer to yourself as God? As you grow into an adult, you no longer need your Earthly father to hold your hand. As you grow into spiritual maturity, you'll no longer need a spiritual father to hold your hand and guide you spiritually. Your Father in Heaven is the only one you will ever need. The only teacher you need is Jesus Christ.

God has a word for you self-righteous preachers: You are worse than hypocrites! Your lives and your teachings are roadblocks to God's kingdom. You refuse to enter, and won't let anyone else in either.

God has something to tell you seminary trained self-righteous hypocrites: You put on a good show for men by sending missionaries all around the world to make converts; but once you convert them, you make them into replicas of yourselves... then you dare to call them Christians after turning them into empty vessels of hell.

You are so blinded by your own ridiculous rules! You say "If a Christian simply makes a promise to you, it doesn't really mean she has to keep her word, or else!" But then you turn right around and say "If she laid her hand on the Bible and swore to keep her promise, then she is bound by that oath. How blind can you be! Are you making the words that are written about me in the Bible more important than the person that I actually live inside of? And what about this piece of nonsense: You say "If you shake hands on a promise, that's nothing; but if you raise your hand and say 'I swear to God' then you had better be telling the truth!" How ludicrous! What's the difference in raising your hand or shaking hands? A promise is a promise. It doesn't matter where you stood, how you had your fingers crossed, whether you were in church at the time, or any other ridiculous rule. What comes out of your mouth is what's in your heart. If you have to have your hand on the Bible before you can tell the truth, then you have the heart of a liar... not my heart.

"You swarm of religious liars! You make sure that everyone around you sees you tithe, because you call it "God's law" ; but the important parts of God's true law, things like love and mercy, justice, fairness and honesty; you don't even consider. There is nothing wrong with tithing.... but you should do it without neglecting the more important things. You are such a hypocrite! "I can't believe that high school couple stole kisses all through church service!" You complain to the woman you're having an affair with.

"You hypocrites! You have your lawn manicured, plant your pretty flower gardens and pull out all the weeds until your house is the envy of the neighborhood; and then you go inside and scream at your children and swear at your husband! If you clean up your home on the inside, then the outside being pretty would actually mean something.

Mausoleums are beautiful structures to behold, indeed. With their elegant carvings and imported marble, they are beautiful to look at on the outside; but inside, they are full of rotting corpses. This is how you are. You go to church wearing a nicely pressed suit or an expensive dress that matches your Bible case. Neighbors look at you and think that you are such good people... but inside you're corrupt and full of gossip and lies.

You're Frauds! You build granite mausoleums for your preachers and marble monuments for your overseers. You say: "If I had lived in the days of Jesus, I would have never been one who called out for his crucifixion." The lady doth protest too much, methinks!" You're cut from the very same cloth as those murderers, and you add to the spiritual death count every day."

"You are Snakes and vipers! Do you think you can buy your way out of this? It's because of people like you that I send true prophets and apostles generation after generation—and every time you treat them like dirt, greeting them with lynch mobs, hounding them with abuse, and telling your church members not to listen to them… because "They are a cult".

"You can't squirm out of this! You'll pay for every drop of righteous blood ever spilled on this Earth from A to Z. Beginning with the blood of Abel right down to the blood of Zechariah, whom you murdered while he was praying; from the blood I shed on the cross to the blood of my missionaries will be on your head! All this, I'm telling you, is coming down on you, and your generation.

"You Church of self-righteous murderers! Murderers of prophets and apostles! Killers of the ones who brought you my love! How often I've ached to embrace you, and you wouldn't let me. And now look at you! You are so desolate that you're nothing but empty shells. What is there left to say? Only this: "Turn from your chains of religion and seek a relationship with me with all of your heart, and I'll show myself to you. But, continue to fight against my Kingdom, and keep even one of my little ones from entering; and one day your knees will shatter and your throat will bleed from screaming my praise".

For this reason also, God highly exalted Him, and bestowed on Him the name which is above every name, so that at the name of Jesus EVERY KNEE WILL BOW, of those who are in Heaven and on Earth and under the Earth, and that every tongue will confess that Jesus Christ is Lord, to the glory of God the Father - Philippians 2:9-11 (New American Standard Bible).

It is the Lord's Prayer that asks that the Kingdom come down to Earth and operate just as it does in Heaven. Several times throughout the book of Matthew Jesus instructs us in prayer, but Matthew Chapter six is the only recorded time that Jesus told us the actual words to say. Don't you think that it should merit more of our attention than simply having the congregation read it aloud together from time to time? The Kingdom refers to the Kingdom of God. You've always known that it is the ultimate goal of a Christian to be able to enter into the Kingdom of God, but what does that mean? Does it mean going to Heaven when you die? Or could it mean something else? Could it have multiple meanings?

Maybe there is something more to this Kingdom than what you've always thought? Did you recognize the writing in this addendum? These are the words that Jesus spoke about the churches and the preachers in Matthew chapter 23. I've only updated it to reflect our society and ways of life. If you became angry or came under conviction while reading, then perhaps it's time for you to take stock of your life. Remember, those are the words of Jesus. If they at first offended me, once I learned that they were His words, I would fall on my face and cry out to Him.

It's a sad but true commentary on the religious world, that even tithing is used as a tool to control pastors. If church boards do not get what they want from a pastor, they will withhold tithes in an effort to "starve out" the pastor, as the pastoral salary usually comes from the tithe. I watched in dismay as a denominational church that I attended in the past not only did this very thing, but bragged about it. I pray for you dear brother. I pray for you sweet sister. I pray that these words would burn in your heart, and that the flames would eat away all of the religious pride until you've been left empty. Once you are empty, you will become a vessel that He can fill. Once you have been filled with the Spirit and with love, you can start to pursue a relationship with your Creator. Once He has set you free, you'll be free indeed. Then you'll know what the Christian life is truly meant to be. When you fall in love, everything changes. Everything becomes wonderful. The walk is no longer hard, and you'll no longer have to struggle with trying to be religious. My prayer for you is the same prayer that Jesus taught us to pray... that you allow yourself to see the Kingdom of Heaven invade Earth.

I know that there are those who like to know the ending before they read through the book, so they will be looking at this paragraph first. To those people, let me state that it will not work in this particular book. You cannot read the last paragraph and figure out the ending. As a matter of fact, if you read this entire addendum before reading the book, you will be doing yourself an incredible injustice. This addendum gives you no semblance whatsoever of the book. Neither does the first addendum, neither does the previous chapter. If you want to know who the winner is... it is you! However, there are no shortcuts. You cannot start at the ending, and you cannot start in the middle. Before you can enter the Kingdom, you have to know that there is such a thing. When you come to see that that there really is a door, you have to have the keys. You only get the keys one way. There is no single paragraph, or a single chapter or even a combination of chapters that will give you the knowledge that you need. You need to start at the beginning and read through to the end. If you've already done that, then let me welcome you to your new Christian walk, because that's exactly what it will be. You will find your new knowledge of the Kingdom life tantamount to your born-again experience. It's that dramatic! Come visit us at www.kingdomcultureministries.org for some more insight and fellowship in your area, and help advance the kingdom of God by spreading the word.

All my love,

Pinky

Recommended Reading

For those who want to know the heart of the Father I HIGHLY recommend:
The Shack by William P. Young www.theshackbook.com

For those who desire to know the historical truth about the life and death of Jesus in their heads as well as their hearts, history becomes His story in:
More Than a Carpenter by Josh and Sean McDowell www.josh.org

For those who desire a practical guide to Bible Study:
How to Study Your Bible by Arthur and DeLacy isbn 978-0-7369-2682-9

For those who desire an intellectual, collegiate level study of the Reformation:
The Age of Reform 1250-1550 by Steven Ozment yalepress.yale.edu/book.asp?isbn=0300027605

For those who desire a stronger foundation, this book examines 42 different passages that can cause problems if we fail to understand them correctly:
Cracks in the Foundation by Steve Backlund www.ignitedhope.com

I would also highly recommend any book by any Bethel author: www.ibethel.org/store/
Including:

For those desiring supernatural witnessing: *The Ultimate Treasure Hunt by Kevin Dedmon*

For those who have the heart of an intercessor: *The Happy Intercessor by Beni Johnson*

For those who have children: *Loving Our Kids on Purpose by Danny Silk*

For those in leadership in the family, church, business etc: *Culture of Honor by Danny Silk*

For those desiring to grow in Kingdom truths: *Any book by Bill Johnson or Kris Vallotton*
Bill is grounded in Kingdom teaching, and anointed to powerfully reveal Kingdom truths.
Kris is prophetic, and pours out insightful revelations with humor and anecdotes.

Endnotes

1. Friend Of God (I Am A Friend Of God) Michael Gungor, Israel Houghton ©2003 Integrity's Praise! Music Vertical Worship Songs All rights reserved. International copyright secured.

2. A few lines are excerpts from Abbott and Costello's famous comedic dialogue entitled "Who's on first?" cir. 1936. First known copyright: 1944.

Printed in the United States
by Baker & Taylor Publisher Services